C0-ALT-469

CAKE DECORATING

SUGAR CRAFT

Marie Sykes & Patricia Simmons

Book No. 3 in the Child & Henry Cake Decorating Series recognised and used by decorators throughout the world.

CAKE DECORATING
SUGAR CRAFT

Marie Sykes
&
Patricia Simmons

C&H CHILD & HENRY

Acknowledgements

We would like to express our thanks for practical help to Norman Nicholls (photography), Charles Stoker (photography), Offray (whose ribbons we use exclusively) and A. F. Bambach Pty Ltd (whose wires we use exclusively).

We would also like to thank Ken Sykes for his patience, perseverance and support.

Published by
Child & Henry Publishing Pty Ltd
9 Clearview Place Brookvale, NSW, Australia, 2100
First Edition, 1985
© Patricia Simmons and Marie Sykes 1985
Typeset by Walter Deblaere and Associates
Printed by Colourwork Press Pte Ltd,
21 Mandai Estate, Singapore
National Library of Australia Card Number and
ISBN 0 86777 074 0
All rights reserved. No part of this publication may be reproduced, stored in a retrieval system, or transmitted in any form or by any means, electronic, mechanical, photocopying, recording, or otherwise, without the prior permission in writing of the publisher.

Jacket photography: Norman Nicholls

Photography: Norman Nicholls and Charles Stoker

CONTENTS

*Cotton net umbrella (page 16) and pearls (page 55) give
interest to this cake. The double flounce adds to its charm*

INTRODUCTION

This book is a companion to our earlier books, *Cake Decorating* and *101 Cake Decorating Ideas*, and should be used with those books. In this book we have provided the decorator with a range of new decorating ideas, using materials, skills and techniques which are not covered in the earlier books.

The chapters on cotton net and nylon tulle decorations give instructions on making a variety of delicate and unusual articles which will add to the visual appeal of cakes for many occasions. We have included a section on using fresh floral arrangements and have given more information on fondant trimmings. Moulded marzipan animals and figures have always been popular with both children and adults, so we have given directions for making many more of these.

Flowers never lose their appeal as one of the traditional cake decorations. In this book we have given full instructions on making wired flowers. This technique is a valuable addition to any decorator's skills and can provide a simple alternative to moulding flowers as described in our earlier books.

Special decorations, such as pearls, cameos and those made with delicate filigree piping, are also covered. A chapter on attractive moulded decorations is included.

All the instructions are given in the fully illustrated easy-to-follow step-by-step format which has proved so successful in our earlier books. The step-by-step photographs of marzipan figures and the wired flowers appear once with the text and again as large plates at the back of the book.

Versatility and creativity are the hallmarks of the successful decorator. This book will give every decorator, whether experienced or a relative newcomer to the craft, added scope for her creative talents.

This unusual wedding cake features wired Australian wildflowers, a delicate frill and cutter embroidery on its sides

Cotton net border (page 12)
and cotton net tiger lilies (page 13)

I
COTTON NET DECORATIONS

A simple and dainty way to highlight a decoration on a cake is to use cotton net. The net must be fine cotton, not nylon, as nylon will not absorb the net stiffener. Here we present a variety of flowers and ornaments which will give a wide choice of decorations. The idea of decorating with cotton net is not new, however it is now becoming popular. It allows the decorator to produce many fine intricate ornaments.

Remember, the net will take on the colour of the icing used.

Here are some general instructions on using cotton net.

Net Stiffener
Cotton net needs to be stiffened so it will retain the desired shape for the decorations. See page 69 for the recipe for net stiffener. This mixture gives good results and will keep for several months if stored in the refrigerator.

Moulds
Cotton net, once it has been stiffened, needs to be shaped into (or onto) a suitable mould so that it dries in the desired shape. Stiffened net is very easy to handle once dry, which makes it a good starting place for the beginner. It will not break easily.

For flowers, small petals can be set into a standard teaspoon; larger petals into a dessertspoon. Various cardboard shapes can be used as moulds for different objects; for example, for the basket on page 19 we used a cardboard cylinder with a diameter of 4 cm (1 ½ in).

Patterns
To cut the net to the desired shape, you will need a suitable pattern for the piece you wish to make. A number of patterns are given in the back of the book. Once you have tried using some of these and have become more experienced you will find you can draw your own.

Making Net Decorations

Step 1: Fold the net (for flowers, approximately six thicknesses) and pin the pattern on firmly to prevent slipping. Cut to the desired shapes.

Step 2: Grease various moulds with *white* vegetable shortening, not butter, margarine or lard as these will discolour the net.

Step 3: Taking a pair of tweezers, dip one net shape into the net stiffener and dab on to a tissue to remove excess moisture.

Step 4: Place over or into the desired mould.

Step 5: While the net is still damp, using No. 0 or 00 tube and medium-peak royal icing, pipe a tiny snail's trail around the net shape, vein and dot as required.

Step 6: Allow to dry.

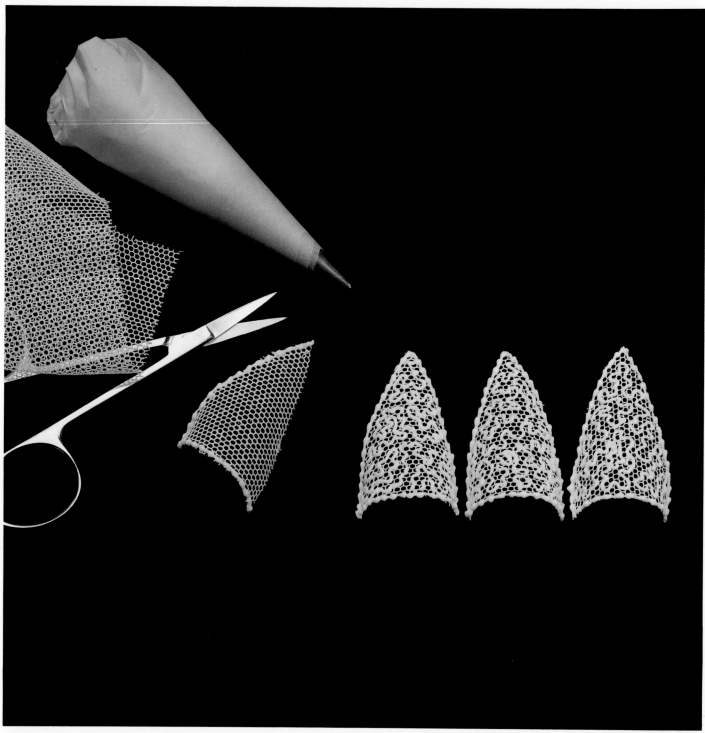

Border

Only cotton net is suitable for this border. The pieces must be stiffened and allowed to dry over a curved surface (such as a broom handle) and then attached to the base of the cake to give a fluted effect. The pieces are triangular in shape; they should be 2.5 cm (1 in) wide at base, and 4 cm (1½ in) deep.

Step 1: Cut the required number of pieces (see pattern, page 85).

Step 2: Dip each shape in the net stiffener, dab out excess moisture and place on a curved surface which has been greased or is covered with plastic film. Using a No. 0 or 00 tube and medium-peak royal icing, embroider as desired while the net is moist.

Step 3: To assemble: Commence piping a shell border (see *ANZ Cake Decorating*), positioning the base of the net into the wet royal icing. Pipe a small dot of icing at the top of the net and attach it to cake. Allow to dry.

Tiger lily

Tiger Lily

Prepare six stamens and one stigma. This flower looks attractive if piped in a bright colour with matching stamen heads.

Step 1: Cut six petals (see pattern, page 83).

Step 2: Grease a curved surface with white vegetable shortening.

Step 3: Taking the tweezers, dip each petal into the net stiffener and dab on a tissue to remove excess moisture.

Step 4: Place over the greased mould.

Step 5: While the net is still damp, using a No. 0 or 00 tube and medium-peak royal icing, pipe a tiny snail's trail. Then vein and dot as required. (Do not pipe dots right up to the tip of the flower.)

Step 6: Allow to dry.

Step 7: To assemble: Assemble the flower in an egg cup. Pipe a small star of firm-peak royal icing in the centre of a square of foil or waxed paper, arrange three petals in a triangle, then a further three petals within the triangle in alternate spaces. Pipe a small star in the centre, adding the stamens and stigma. Allow to dry.

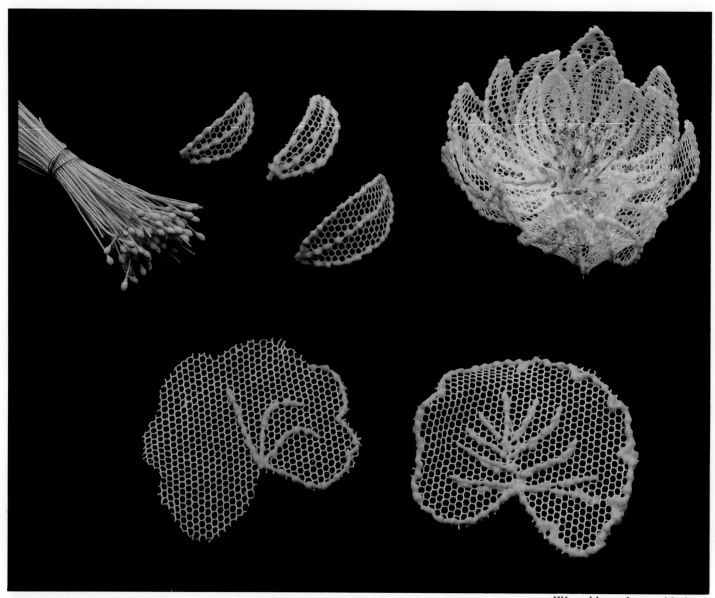

Waterlily and waterlily leaf

Waterlily

With a small doll placed among the stamens, this flower may also be used on a Christening cake.

Step 1: Cut twenty-seven petals (nine in each of three sizes) small, medium and large. (See pattern, page 83).

Step 2: Grease a curved surface with vegetable shortening to use as a mould.

Step 3: Taking the tweezers, dip one shape into the syrup and dab on a tissue to remove excess moisture.

Step 4: Place over prepared mould.

Step 5: While the net is damp, pipe a snail's trail around the edge of the petal and vein, using a No. 0 or 00 tube, and medium-peak royal icing.

Step 6: Allow to dry.

Step 7: To assemble: Take a small square of foil, waxed paper or greased greaseproof paper and pipe a star of firm-peak royal icing. Arrange the nine largest petals evenly in a circle, then add a little more royal icing and place the next row of medium-sized petals in alternate spaces. If necessary add a little more royal icing and then place the small petals in alternate spaces. Finally add the stamens liberally.

Waterlily Leaf

Step 1: Cut several leaves, following pattern on page 83.

Step 2: Grease a flat surface with white vegetable shortening.

Step 3: Using tweezers, dip one shape into the net stiffener and dab on a tissue to remove excess moisture.

Step 4: Place on prepared surface.

Step 5: Pipe a snail's trail around the edge of the leaf, and vein using a No. 0 or 00 tube and medium-peak royal icing.

Step 6: Allow to dry.

Step 7: Use with the flower; arrange as desired.

Briar rose and Christening rose

Briar Rose and Christening Rose

Many flowers can be made using the same method but by varying the patterns and the colours. The briar rose is a single rose. Given two or more rows of petals and a doll placed amongst the stamens, it becomes a Christening rose.

Step 1: Cut five petals (see pattern, page 83) for the briar rose.

Step 2: Grease a dessertspoon or tablespoon with white vegetable shortening, to use as the mould.

Step 3: Taking the tweezers, dip one shape into the net stiffener and dab on a tissue to remove excess moisture.

Step 4: Place over or into the spoon, with the pointed tip set close to the handle.

Step 5: While the net is still damp, using a No. 0 or 00 tube and medium-peak royal icing, pipe a tiny snail's trail and a few veins at the base of the petal.

Step 6: Allow to dry.

Step 7: Repeat for each petal.

Step 8: To assemble: Take a piece of foil or waxed paper, pipe a small star in the centre using firm-peak royal icing. Arrange the petals in a circle, pipe a further small star in the centre and add stamens liberally. Allow to dry.

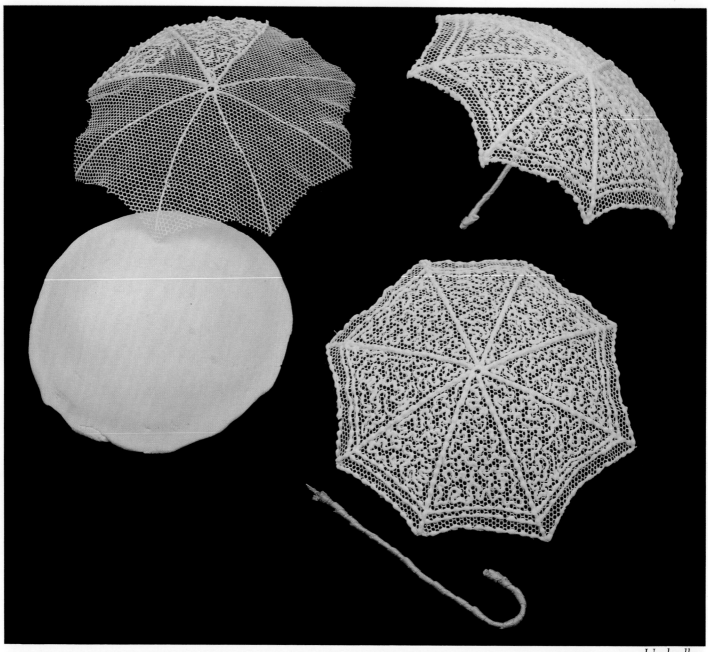

Umbrella

Umbrella

Umbrellas and half umbrellas, decorated with flowers, look most attractive on pre-wedding, shower party and birthday cakes.

Step 1: Use a soup bowl, or saucer, or similar shallow curved object as a mould. Grease with white vegetable shortening.

Step 2: Cut a net circle of suitable size (see pattern, page 84). Fold in half, in half again, and in half again. (This will give you a folded segment of a circle which is one-eighth of a circle.) Cut a shallow concave curve into the curved end.

Step 3: Using tweezers, dip the net shape into the stiffener and dab on a tissue to remove excess moisture.

Step 4: Place over or in the prepared mould.

Step 5: While the net is still damp, using a No. 0 or 00 tube and medium-peak royal icing, pipe from the rim to the centre, leaving a small hole for the wire handle. Complete piping around the edge. Allow to dry.

Step 6: When dry, turn the piece over and overpipe the rims and outer edge for added strength. Allow to dry.

Step 7: Prepare a piece of fine wire for the handle. Wind a narrow ribbon around the handle to within 1 cm (¼ in) of the tip. Place the tip in the centre of the hole in the net shape. Seal it with a spot of royal icing. Cover the tip with royal icing. Allow to dry.

Half Umbrella

The half umbrella is made in the same way as the full umbrella, however it is dried along the side of a 5 cm (2 in) diameter glass jar or tumbler. The handle is placed flat on the cake or board.

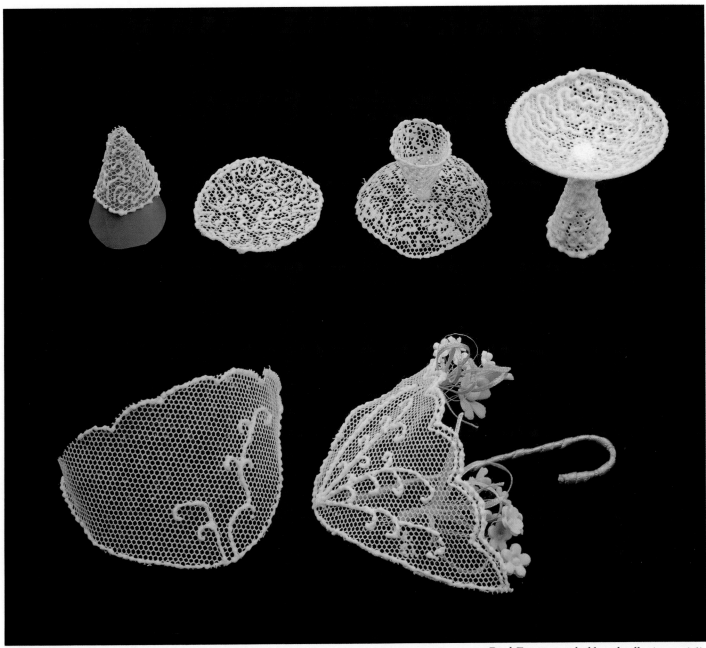

Bird Fountain; half umbrella (page 16)

Bird Fountain

The Stem

Step 1: Using the pattern on page 84, make a cone of greaseproof paper and secure. Cut another cone in cotton net.

Step 2: Grease the paper cone with white vegetable shortening.

Step 3: Dip the net into net stiffener. Dab on tissue to remove excess moisture. Place over the paper cone, making sure that the edges overlap neatly.

Step 4: Using a No. 0 or 00 tube and medium-peak royal icing, pipe around the edge and embroider, or pipe cornelli design. Allow to dry.

The Bowl

Step 5: The bowl. Cut a circle in cotton net for the bowl (see pattern, page 84).

Step 6: Dip the new bowl into the stiffener and dab on tissue to remove excess moisture. Place in a greased shape, such as a round bottomed patty pan.

Step 7: While the net is still damp, using a No. 0 or 00 tube and medium-peak icing, embroider, or pipe cornelli design all over, finishing with a tiny scalloped edge. Allow to dry.

Step 8: To assemble: Carefully snip the point from the tip of the cone and join to the bowl with a spot of royal icing. If necessary fill the cone with foil or cotton wool to support it.

Forget-me-nots, piped on fine green cotton, allowed to dry and placed over the fountain, will give a dainty finish. Piped birds can also be added to the fountain as a finishing touch.

Rattle and pillars

Rattle

Step 1: Mould a handle from modelling fondant, or cover several strands of fine wire with narrow satin ribbon.

Step 2: See photograph for finished rattle. Cut two pieces of net 4 cm (1½ in) long and each piece wide enough to go around half the shape. Cut two circles 2 cm (¾ in) diameter for the ends.

Step 3: Grease the mould with white vegetable shortening. A piece of dowel rod 2 cm (¾ in) in diameter is suitable.

Step 4: Taking the tweezers, dip each net piece into the stiffener and dab on a tissue to remove excess moisture. Place

the long pieces along the mould to curve, and the two circles on to a flat surface. Leave a small hole in the centre of one of the circles for the handle to be inserted.

Step 5: Using a No. 0 or 00 tube and medium-peak royal icing, embroider a nursery motif or cornelli design. Allow to dry.

Step 6: Join the two curved shapes with royal icing and attach the two flat circles to the ends. Insert handle, secure with a little royal icing; prop up with cotton wool if necessary. Finish rattle with a ribbon and bow of a matching colour.

Net pillars are made in the same way as the rattle. Paint the skewers white or bind with ribbon.

18

Basket

Basket

The net basket with a dainty serrated edge is widely used in decorating. The basket is quite strong and yet it appears fragile. Flowers are easily arranged in it without breakage.

Step 1: Cut out the pattern on paper (see page 85) and draw the design on this. Draw the design clearly with dark pencil or biro so it will be visible through a thickness of waxed paper and cotton net.

Step 2: Cut one thickness of net and dip in stiffener. Place the paper pattern under a piece of waxed paper on the mould (a cardboard cylinder would do). Position the net shape over this.

Step 3: Pipe a snail's trail on the net shape around the *edge* of the base and the sides. Following the pattern, fill in the design with a snail's trail. Allow to dry.

Step 4: Remove the net from the mould and overpipe on the back of the basket for added strength. Allow to dry.

Step 5: Shape a piece of covering fondant to fit the base of the basket. Place wired bunched ribbons in the fondant and then add tiny wired flowers and leaves. Place in the basket.

Step 6: Cover a suitable length of fine wire with ribbon for the handle. Place in position using a spot of royal icing to secure. Put a few stitches in the ribbon at each end to ensure firmness.

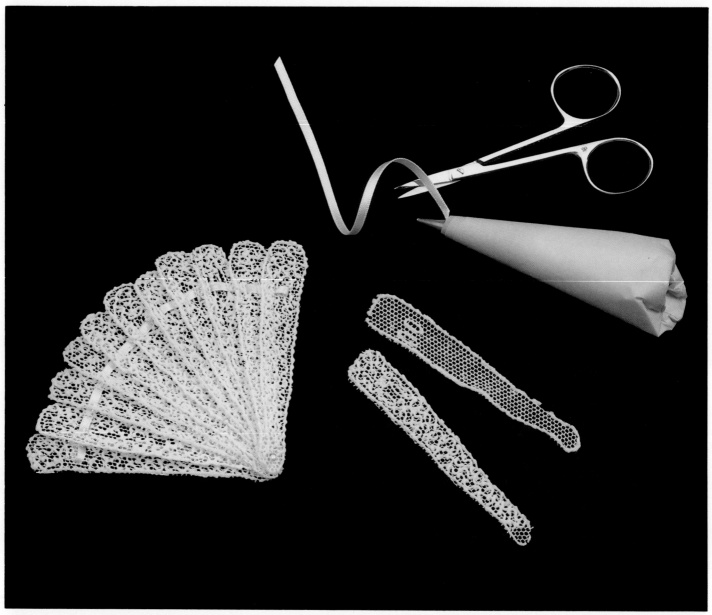

Fan

Fan

The net fan looks most attractive accompanied by a small floral spray or other suitable decoration.

Step 1: Cut ten to seventeen pieces of net (see pattern, page 84, remembering to mark ribbon slots and the pinhole at the base.

Step 2: Dip cotton net pieces in stiffener. Pat excess moisture away and place on a greased flat tray.

Step 3: Pipe a snail's trail around the edges while the net is still damp; fill in with a cornelli design or scrolls, or a floral motif. (As the base of each piece is small, taper off the snail's trail before the base on most pieces. This will give less bulk when assembled.)

Step 4: Thread each piece with a narrow satin ribbon, so that each piece overlaps slightly. Fasten together at the base with a fine stitch and cover the stitch with a pearl stamen dipped in royal icing.

Wheelbarrow

A net barrow, filled with flowers, makes an attractive decoration for various cakes. The barrow may also be filled with fruit or sweets for children's parties.

Step 1: Using firm cardboard to make the mould, cut a barrow base (see pattern, page 85).

Step 2: Bend sides at the base of the cuts, and join A-B, C-D, E-F and G-H. Line with greased greaseproof paper, or plastic film.

Step 3: Cut one barrow base in net, two handles, two legs and one wheel (if there is enough cotton net available, use a double thickness to add strength).

Step 4: Dip the base net into the net stiffener, dab with a tissue to remove excess moisture and place inside the mould. Join A-B, C-D, E-F, G-H. Pipe a snail's trail on the seams and around the edges with medium-peak royal icing using a No. 0 or 00 tube. Embroider the sides of the barrow or pipe a cornelli design and allow to dry. When dry, remove from mould.

Step 5: Dip handles, legs, and wheels in net stiffener and place on *flat* greased greaseproof paper or plastic film. Pipe around with a corresponding design to that used on the base. Allow to dry. Leave a pinhole in the wheel for the shaft. Pipe on both sides for added strength.

Step 6: When dry attach the two handles, the small front wheel and the shaft and legs, as illustrated.

A most attractive ball-shaped cake featuring three fondant
frills in contrasting colours, wired easy carnations (page 48),
leaves (page 45) and a tulle butterfly (page 41)

II
FONDANT TRIMMINGS

Modelling fondant is used for making many decorations including flowers, leaves, bowls and bells. Covering fondant is generally used to cover a cake but it can also be used for making edible ornaments. Modelling fondant holds it shape better than covering fondant.

The fondant frill and wired flowers make this an appealing cake for a very special birthday

Fondant Frill

The fondant frill is a very effective method of decorating the base of a cake. An upside-down frill is similar to a ruffle and can be used along the top edge of a cake. Frills can also be used to decorate a ball cake.

Step 1: Roll out strips of covering fondant about 2.5 cm (1 in) wide and 9 cm (3½ in) long.

Step 2: Trim one edge carefully with a pastry cutter or scalloped cutter.

Step 3: Frill the edges by rolling a small modelling stick to and fro about 1.25 cm (½ in) in from the edge.

Step 4: Attach the frill to the cake by dampening the straight edge with egg white or water and placing in position. If using as an upside-down frill, position the frill with the frilled edge uppermost. A double frill, in two colours, is very attractive. Neaten the straight edge with a pastry cutter, small flower cutters or crimpers.

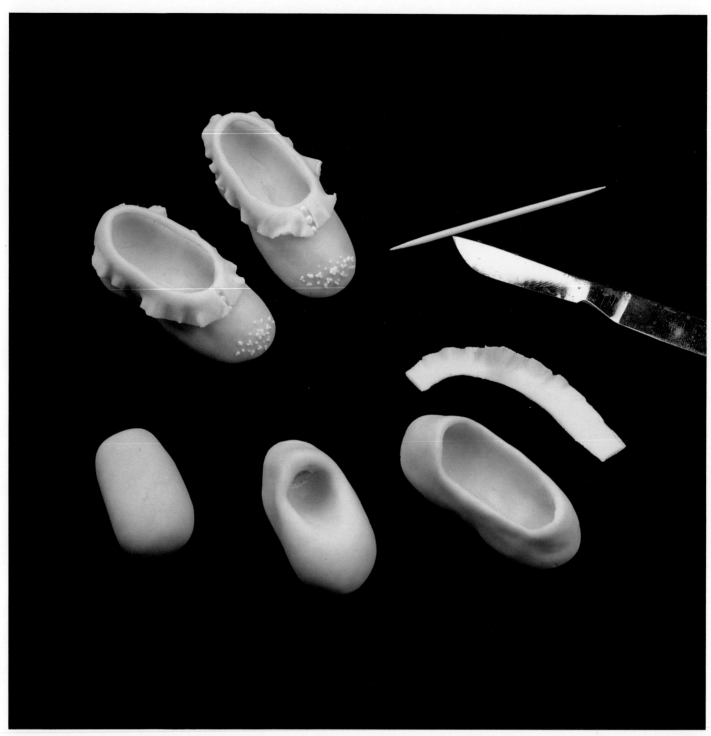

Bootees

Fondant bootees can be used to decorate Christening cakes. They may be finished with a little bow, or piped with forget-me-nots, or a tiny nursery design may be piped on the front of the bootee. Bootees are often arranged with a spray of tiny flowers.

Step 1: Take a small ball of covering fondant (or modelling fondant if they are to be kept as a memento). Shape into an oblong.

Step 2: Using a ball-end spike (similar to hair roller spikes), hollow out the oblong, working around it to form the sides and the back of the bootees.

Step 3: Roll out paste very thinly and cut two small straps. Make one end pointed and put a slit in it to form a buttonhole. Insert a pearl stamen in the other end for the button.

Step 4: While the fondant is still soft, attach the strap, using egg white or water.

Step 5: Repeat the process to make another bootee, taking care that they do actually match.

Step 6: When thoroughly dry, using a No. 0 or 00 tube, pipe a suitable design of cornelli, or miniature basket weave to resemble crochet, or a tiny spray in contrasting colours.

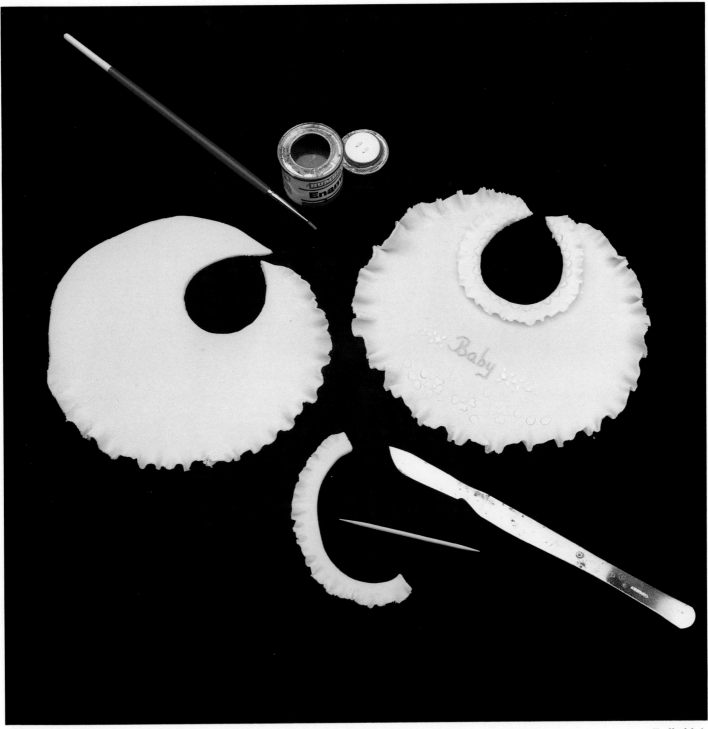

Frilled Bib

If covering fondant is used, the bib may be cut when the cake is cut. If you use modelling fondant, the bib may be kept as a memento.

Step 1: Cut a bib in covering or modelling fondant (see pattern, page 86).

Step 2: Frill the edges by rolling a cocktail stick to and fro about 1 cm (¼ in) in from the edge. Apply pressure firmly on the edge of the fondant.

Step 3: Decorate with piped nursery figures and small flowers, or flood small motifs on the bib.

A posy featuring frangipani and maidenhair fern on an
undecorated cake. See page 28 for the step-by-step photograph

III
FLORAL ARRANGEMENTS

Often a request is made for fresh flower decorations on wedding cakes instead of sugar flowers. On the other hand, good quality artificial flowers may be used where seasons, areas or climates prevent the use of fresh flowers. They are everlasting.

A florist will readily make up a posy of fresh flowers for the cake to match the bridal bouquet, but it is more satisfying (and economical) to make your own.

Fresh flowers can make a lovely alternative to sugar flowers

Fresh Flowers for Decoration on Cakes

We have illustrated stephanotis, frangipani, Cecil Brunner roses and fairy roses, all with maidenhair fern. Any small dainty flowers may be used, or a combination of several can be used in mixed posies.

Choose flowers that will not wilt easily. Pick them early in the morning or in the late evening on the day before. Stand the flowers in a container of water right up to the blooms, as they require a long drink before handling.

When ready to wire, handle the flowers firmly, but as little as possible. Use wires sparingly and wind only in the one direction.

Fresh flowers for decoration on cakes; Cecil Brunner roses, fairy roses and maidenhair fern

Fresh flowers for decoration on cakes; top: stephanotis and maidenhair fern; above: frangipani and maidenhair fern

Step 1: Take a piece of 26 gauge florist's wire, pierce the base of flower, bending the wire to form a hairpin loop. Twist it around the base of the flower, bending it over the hairpin loop.

Step 2: Wire as many flowers as required, including buds, fine ferns and ribbon loops.

Step 3: Once all pieces are wired, cover one third of the wire from the base of the flower with parafilm or florist's tape, stretching it finely as far as possible.

Step 4: Select five to seven wired flowers, arrange them in a circle and twist all wires to form a wire handle. Hold the posy upright while working; top in all other blooms, buds, net and ribbon loops within the circle.

Step 5: Tighten all wires into the handle. Remove surplus wire, leaving a small handle.

Step 6: Tape the handle carefully with parafilm or florist's tape stretched finely as possible. This small handle can be placed into a flower spike or directly into the cake or a small vase may be used instead of a flower spike.

Fresh flowers are not left on the cake for longer than the occasion demands. Parafilm-covered wires will not damage the cake in any way for this short time.

Courtesy of Leona Charlwood.

*Floral arrangements on fondant foundations; from the left:
spray, crescent and posy*

Floral Arrangements on Fondant Foundations

First of all decide whether your arrangement is to be a posy,
a crescent, or a spray. Use a small fondant foundation: a posy
has a small ball-shaped foundation, about the size of a wal-
nut; a crescent has a half-moon shaped one; a spray a carrot-
shaped one. Remember to keep the fondant foundation
small; the larger the shape the more flowers will be needed.

Step 1: Prepare all wired flowers, buds, leaves, ribbon loops
and tulle fans (if required).

Step 2: Using a small portion of matching coloured covering
fondant, roll the foundation into the desired shape.

Step 3: Set the foundation in position on the cake and allow
to stand for 24 hours before commencing to decorate, as this
will be easier to work on.

Step 4: Arrange ribbon loops in position.

Step 5: Position feature flowers (roses, frangipani,
stephanotis, etc).

Step 6: Top in with smaller flowers and buds, using hyacinth
and bouvardia, etc., for lightness.

Step 7: Fill in underneath with small flowers and leaves,
adjust flowers and ribbons if required with tweezers.

Step 8: If an extra ribbon loop is required to fill a space, insert
it carefully.

Class No. 302
Catalogue No. 3322
(Pin or Stick on Exhibit)

Kermit and Miss Piggy

IV
MOULDING WITH MARZIPAN

Moulding with marzipan is an old form of sugar art. Various shapes can be used and colours play a big part in their presentation. Also, as an added bonus, marzipan decorations are edible.

Many animals, figures and flowers are suitable and make popular simple decorations for sponge and butter cakes. See the recipe for marzipan used for modelling. 'Animals' features, such as eyes, nose and paws, can be given colour emphasis with a very light touch of melted chocolate, applied with a fine brush.

Kermit and Miss Piggy

Step 1: Mould Kermit's body using green-coloured marzipan, covering fondant, or a mixture of modelling and covering fondants and push a satay stick into the neck, leaving enough stick protruding to secure his head. Allow to dry.

Step 2: Mould the head using the same material, in the same colour. (See pattern, page 88). Cut a slit for his mouth and slightly ease out his lower lip. Place the head on the satay stick. Allow to dry.

Step 3: Mould long narrow arms and legs and allow to dry. Attach to the body using a little royal icing.

Step 4: Cover head, body, legs and arms with bright green royal icing that has been thinned down with a little water or egg white. Allow to dry.

Step 5: Mould a peaked collar with the fondant and attach with royal icing.

Step 6: Mould eyes and paint on details; allow to dry. Attach to head with a little royal icing.

Miss Piggy
Miss Piggy is moulded in a similar way, but we suggest that her head be made of fondant only, as a royal icing cover is then not necessary. Dress her as pictured.

Courtesy of Margaret Tesoriero.

Rose and Leaf

Step 1: Take a ball of marzipan about the size of a 10 cent piece, bring the top to a point and press a waist into the centre, leaving the balance to fan out and form a stand.

Step 2: Dust your forefinger and thumb lightly with cornflour and gently squeeze from the pointed top, down one-third of the bud, to form a small flag. Using a paintbrush moistened with egg white or water, brush the flag and wrap it around the tip to give a spiral effect. This is now the tight bud, the centre of the rose.

Rose and leaf

Step 3: Mould a small petal and wrap it about one-third of the way round the bud; secure it (and all other petals) at the base with a spot of egg white or water. Mould two more petals slightly larger in size and attach them. Mould a fourth petal; it begins to open on one side of the bud. It and subsequent petals are made in a teardrop shape and fingered out as finely as possible on the top edges. Press over the forefinger to give shape and attach each petal overlapping the previous petal by about one-third until the desired shape is achieved.

Step 4: Mould sepals: Make a basic hollow cone, cut into five long equal parts and mitre each sepal. Leaves are moulded freehand, veined with the back of a knife and given a slight twist for a realistic look.

Step 5: When the rose is complete, cut the base off carefully with a knife or scissors to make a neat finish. Set for at least 24 hours in a patty tin and store away from dust.

Kangaroo and Joey

Step 1: Take a ball of grey marzipan about the size of a golf ball and shape it into a sausage shape with one end pointed, and the other left blunt.

Step 2: On the pointed end cut one incision a little way down from the point on each side. Shape upwards to form the ears.

Kangaroo and Joey

Step 3: Cut two more incisions about one-third of the way down and mould for the two front paws.

Step 4: Cut one incision on either side of the blunt end for the back legs, leaving the balance to form the tail. Mould into shape, giving the tail a curl. (The kangaroo will balance on his back legs and tail.)

Step 5: Insert eyes and nose in a dark colour.

Step 6: Make the joey: Mould a tiny head, ears and eyes in a contrasting colour. With a pointed tool, make a hole in the kangaroo for the pouch and insert the joey, using a little egg white or water so it will attach firmly.

Elephant

Colour the marzipan a grey colour by using green and brown colours.

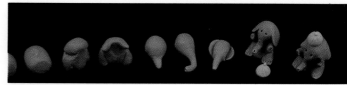

Elephant

Step 1: Take a ball of marzipan and mould it to an elongated shape.

Step 2: Cut two shallow slits for the back legs and, on the other end, two rounded slits for the front legs.

Step 3: Mould the back legs to sit forward, and the front legs to curve forward (this elephant is sitting on his haunches). Mark toenails.

Step 4: Take a smaller ball of marzipan and mould the head and trunk, cut two small rounded slits for the ears. Mould into shape. Pierce the eyes with a cocktail stick. Moisten and attach to the body.

Step 5: Mould a tiny beret in a contrasting colour and place in position.

Snake

Step 1: Take a piece of green coloured marzipan and roll it out to a long thin shape until it is about 30 cm (12 in) long.

Step 2: Cut a mouth on one end and add a small pink tongue. Taper the other end.

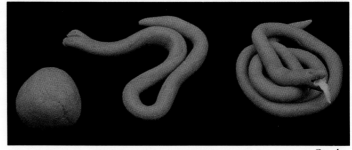

Snake

Step 3: Curl the snake around with its head looking towards the front. Pierce two small eyes with a cocktail stick.

Tortoise

Step 1: Take a ball of marzipan and roll it out tapered at each end, but leave it fat in the middle.

Step 2: Cut two shallow slits about 2.5 cm (1 in) from the tips of each end (four cuts altogether).

Step 3: Curve the slits away from the body, to give the impression of the front and back legs.

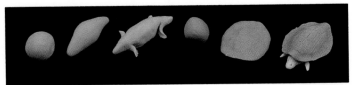

Step 4: Mark two tiny eyes for the head.

Step 5: Take another piece of marzipan in a contrasting colour and mould the shell in an oval shape. Mark the shell with a suitable tool and place in position over the body. The head and tail just peep out from the shell.

Pig

Step 1: Take a ball of pink marzipan; pull two ears up and pull a snout out. Mark the eyes with a cocktail stick.

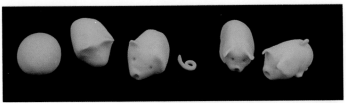

Pig

Step 2: Mark two slanted shallow strips to resemble the front legs and two for the back legs.

Step 3: Mould a tiny curled tail; attach in position with egg white or water.

Mouse

Step 1: Take a small ball of marzipan and mould one part to a point, leaving the roundness for its body.

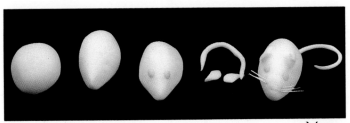

Mouse

Step 2: Mark the eye sockets and insert a tiny ball of pink marzipan in each.

Step 3: Add white stamen cottons for whiskers.

Step 4: Mould a long tail separately. Give it a curl and place in position with a little water or egg white. The tail is fragile when rolled out finely, so care must be taken when handling.

Step 5: Mould two tiny pointed ears and attach to the head.

Snail

Step 1: Take a piece of coloured marzipan and roll it out to resemble a slug, tapering the ends.

Step 2: Make a 1.25 cm (½ in) slit in one end and pull up two small feelers. Place small balls of marzipan on the top of the feelers for the eyes.

Snail

Step 3: Take a contrasting colour (or two colours), mould in a sausage shape and then role to resemble a shell. Attach in position on the body with a little egg white or water.

Duck

Step 1: Take a ball of yellow marzipan and pinch out a rounded flat piece for the tail.

Step 2: Slash the tail section to resemble feathers.

Step 3: Take a smaller ball for the head and pinch out a beak. Mark the eyes and attach the head to the body.

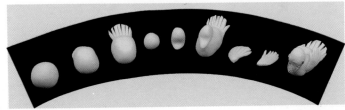

Duck

Step 4: Place tiny balls of a dark colour in position for the eyes. Mould a darker piece and attach to the beak to make a bill.

Step 5: Cut a pair of wings, feather, and attach to the body.

Frog

Step 1: Take a ball of green coloured marzipan and press two indentations for the eyes, shape the wide mouth, and mark two shallow cuts for the front legs.

Step 2: Press the two front legs forward, while rounding the stomach.

Step 3: Cut a slit in the mouth to open and place a small quantity of pink coloured marzipan inside. Line the eye sockets with lighter coloured marzipan.

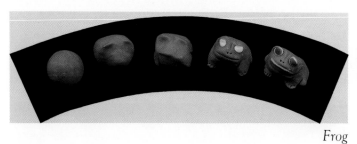

Frog

Step 4: Pierce two small holes, just a little above the mouth for nostrils and add two small balls of a dark colour in the eye socket over the light colour.

Step 5: Shape the back legs, marking them with a knife, pulling them out slightly to give the appearance of a frog squatting.

Alligator or Crocodile

Step 1: Take a ball of marzipan in a suitable colour and mould to a sausage shape with tapered ends.

Step 2: Split one end in halves for the mouth and taper the other end further for the tail.

Step 3: Pinch the back, and indent with a suitable tool for the skin markings.

Alligator or crocodile

Step 4: Insert round balls for the bulging eyes and pipe sharp white teeth to the open mouth.

Step 5: Roll four small pieces for the legs, marking claws on each piece with a knife.

Step 6: Attach legs in position with a little water or egg white.

Seal

Step 1: Take a ball of marzipan and roll it out to a sausage shape with the ends tapered.

Step 2: Split one end 1.25 cm (½ in) and open in a 'V' shape for the tail.

Step 3: Cut two rounded slits about 2.5 cm (1 in) in from the other tip, curve back for the front flippers (the piece in the middle becomes the head).

Seal

Step 4: Shape the head and nose to point upwards, mark eyes with a cocktail stick.

Step 5: Mould a small coloured ball and balance on the tip of the nose (moisten with egg white or water to attach).

Father Christmas Head

Step 1: Roll out a piece of pink coloured marzipan for the head and elongate it.

Step 2: Roll out a small piece in red; shape as a basic hollow cone for the hat; pull the tip a little longer and give it a slight curl. (Alternatively the hat may be made in another colour and painted red.)

Father Christmas head

Step 3: Roll out a flat piece of marzipan and cut the edge to give it a fur-like look. Add this piece to the edge of the hat.

Step 4: Add the hat to the pink head, marking the eyes with a cocktail stick. Place tiny balls of brown in position for the eyes and a small ball of red for the nose.

Step 5: Roll out and cut a beard and moustache. Attach to the head.

Gnome

Step 1: Take a ball of green marzipan, finger to an elongated shape.

Step 2: Cut one end about 2.5 cm (1 in) to resemble the trouser legs.

Step 3: Add two small brown pointed shoes to the trousers.

Step 4: Roll out a piece of yellow marzipan and drape over the shoulders (top part of green shape).

Step 5: Roll out two arms in yellow marzipan and place a pair of brown gloves on the end of each.

Step 6: Attach the arms with a little egg white or water.

Step 7: Mould a pink ball for the head and a tiny brown hat (using the basic hollow cone method) and place on the pink ball.

Step 8: Mark eyes and nose and place a small ball of dark marzipan in each eye. Mark the nostrils with a cocktail stick.

Step 9: Make a beard and moustache and attach to the head.

Step 10: Attach the head to the body with a little egg white or water.

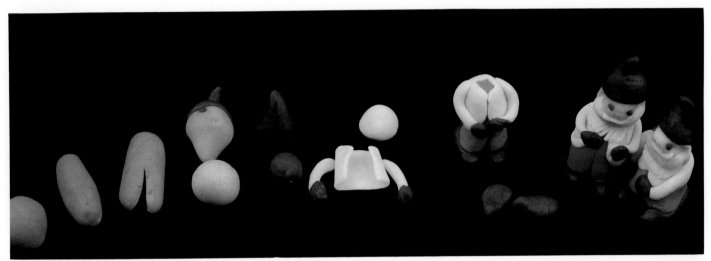

Gnome

*Nylon tulle dress (page 38) combines with pinks, wild violets
and eriostemon to present a delightful Christening cake*

V
NYLON TULLE DECORATIONS

Fine nylon tulle does not require stiffening. Tulle bows, dresses, handkerchiefs, butterflies and leaves are some dainty decorations which will give a light and airy appearance. If the piping is neatly done with a fine tube, tulle work can be the feature of the cake.

Piping may be done in pastel colours to match the cake or in contrasting colour. Care should be taken to allow the piping to dry thoroughly, then it must be handled gently to avoid breakage.

Pipe with soft-peak icing. If a medium- or firm-peak icing is used, it will break away from the tulle. Piping on tulle is usually done over waxed paper. As fine tulle is very hard to see, pin a dark-coloured piece of paper behind the waxed paper before commencing to embroider.

Nylon tulle handkerchief (page 38)

Dress

Dress

Remember to keep the size of the dress in proportion to the size of the cake!

Step 1: Cut a tulle bodice of two thicknesses (see pattern, page 90). Cut a skirt about 16 cm (6¼ in) wide and 12 cm (4¾ in) deep. With fine stitching, gather the top of the skirt; fold the bodice over and stitch to the skirt.

Step 2: Pin a piece of waxed paper under each surface to be embroidered. Use your own design and keep it simple – do not overdecorate.

Step 3: Finish the hemline with a dainty scallop. Handle with extreme care when dry as this is very fragile.

Handkerchief

Tulle handkerchiefs may be used on a cake with a spray of flowers and/or pearls, for many celebrations, including weddings, Christenings, birthdays and special occasions.

Step 1: Cut a piece of tulle about 20 cm (8 in) square.

Step 2: Fold the tulle cornerwise, with one centre peak longer than the other and secure with pins.

Step 3: Fold the side pieces over towards the centre in soft drapes, leaving space for design to show.

Step 4: Pin a piece of dark-coloured paper under the waxed paper pinned to the tulle before commencing to pipe the design.

Step 5: Using soft-peak icing and a No. 0 or 00 tube, pipe your special design in the corner. Finish the edges with a dainty scallop, either small or large. Remove both pieces of paper. Place a spray of flowers over the pinned corner.

Bow

Bow

Step 1: Cut five pieces of tulle (see pattern, page 86) and five pieces of waxed paper to match.

Step 2: Make two loops to form the main part of the bow. Pin the matching pieces of tulle and waxed paper together to form a loop. Repeat to form a second loop. Pipe a tiny snail's trail around the edges; fill in with dots or any suitable design. Stand the loops on their sides to dry.

Step 3: Pipe the two tail pieces as a pair in a matching design and dry flat on waxed paper.

Step 4: Pipe the remaining small centrepiece in the same way, drying it over a skewer covered with waxed paper or foil.

Step 5: To assemble: Handling with extreme care, remove the waxed paper from the loops. Pipe a small star of royal icing, place the two loops into the icing with the tips meeting in the centre. Pipe another small star in the centre and attach tail pieces. Place the small centrepiece in position with a spot of royal icing. Allow to dry.

*Fluted tulle border decorates this cake, which also features
roses and leaves*

Fluted Tulle Border

The tulle border is a dainty finish to a cake, giving it a very
soft look. The border may be used for wedding cakes, Christening cakes or a girl's birthday cake.

Step 1: Cut a long narrow strip 2.5 cm (1 in) wide of tulle
about three times the circumference of the cake. Gather,
using small stitches. Place the tulle around the cake, so that
the bottom edge is just above the board.

Step 2: Secure the tulle to the base of the cake by piping a
small spot of icing at regular intervals, allowing the tulle to
flute. It may be necessary to pin it in position until the icing
is dry.

Step 3: Using soft-peak royal icing, and a No. 0 or 00 tube,
pipe in cornelli or a suitable design. The lower edge may be
finished with a tiny scallop, snail's trail or zigzag, the top
edge finished with piped-on lace or ribbon (or both) to cover
the gathering, or both.

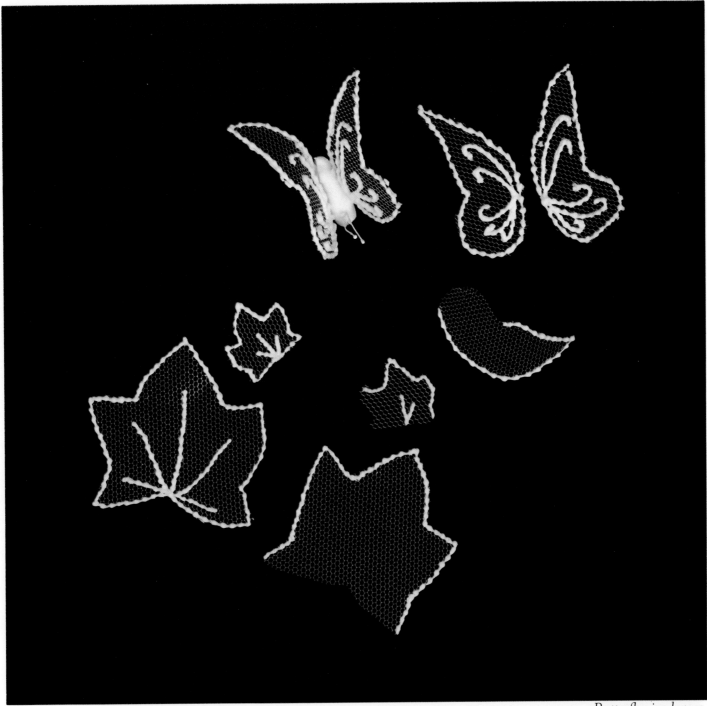

Butterfly

Tulle butterflies look very dainty on Christening and wedding cakes. They may be tinted or white.

Step 1: Cut a pair of wings (see pattern, page 90) and pipe a tiny snail's trail around the edges, using a No. 0 or 00 tube. Embroider wings as desired. Allow to dry on a flat surface.

Step 2: Using firm-peak royal icing and a No. 5 star tube, pipe a small shell for the head, a slightly larger shell for the thorax, and a longer section for the body.

Step 3: Attach dried wings to the thorax and support if necessary.

Step 4: Curve two stamens for the antennae and insert into the head section. Allow to dry.

Ivy Leaves

Tulle leaves are a dainty addition to cakes if piped finely and kept to a small size. (For ivy, rose and waterlily leaf patterns, see page 83).

Step 1: Prepare a piece of waxed paper, or plastic film.

Step 2: Cut a few leaves at one time.

Step 3: Using soft-peak royal icing and a No. 0 or 00 tube, pipe a tiny zigzag edge around the leaf and pipe veins.

Step 4: Allow to dry.

Leaves may be piped over a slightly curved surface for effect.

A posy of wired flowers, featuring easy carnations (page 48),
snowflake, hyacinth and cutter flowers (page 45)

VI
MAKING WIRED FLOWERS

There are times when it is easier to wire the petals and leaves of many flowers as they can then be moved without breakage. Using wired flowers can be very convenient when assembling a spray. However, do try other methods, such as assembling with royal icing, and use the one most suitable to your needs. Wires must be strong enough to support the petals, but fine enough to wind into a neat and slender stem.

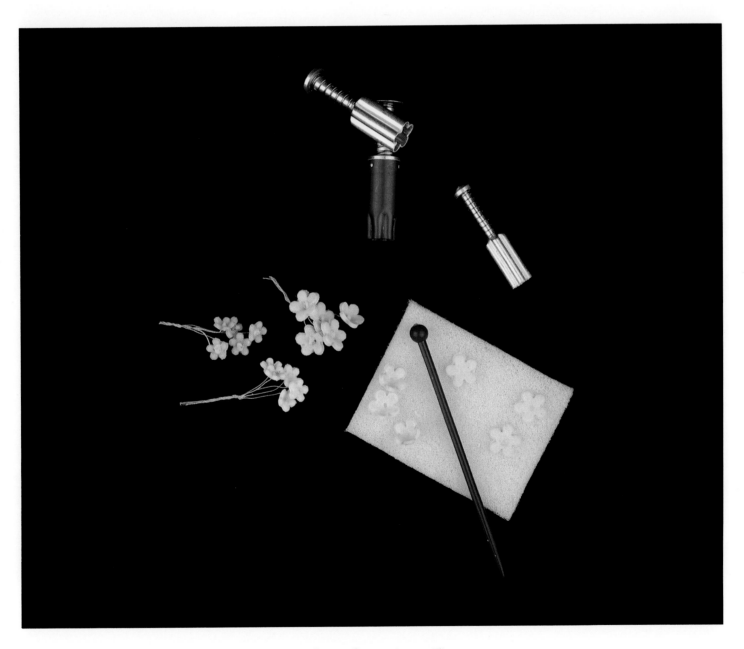

Cutter flowers (page 45)

43

Wired leaves.
Seen here, clockwise from the right, are geranium, rose, holly,
pelargonium, chrysanthemum, ivy and maple leaves. Patterns
are given on page 83. You can use this method to make any
leaves you may require

Cutter Flowers

The use of cutters is a quick and easy way of making small flowers. Most cutters, including spring-centre cutters, are readily available in cake decorating supply shops. The small flowers made in this way are very attractive.

Step 1: Roll out a piece of modelling fondant as finely as possible. Cut a number of small shapes. Cover all the shapes, except the one that you are working on.

Step 2: Place the shape on a piece of foam rubber and cup with a round-end modelling stick or the spring-centre of the cutter.

Step 3: With a fine needle, pierce the centre. Allow to dry.

Step 4: Dip stamen head into thinned down royal icing and pull through centre into position. Allow to dry.

Step 5: Buds may be made by dipping stamen heads into thinned down royal icing and allowed to dry. Calyxes may be painted on the buds if required.

Step 6: To assemble: Take one or two buds and two or three flowers, bind with fine wire and cover with parafilm or florist's tape that has been cut into several strips.

Petals and Leaves

Step 1: Take a ball of fondant of suitable size, dip the wire into egg white or water, insert the wire into the centre of the ball and roll out finely.

Step 2: Using a cutter or pattern, stamp or cut to the desired shape.

Step 3: Finger cut edges, vein and flute, or ruffle as required. Give the petal or leaf a twist or curve, rather than leaving to dry flat. This gives a more natural appearance.

Step 4: Wind a thin strip of parafilm or florist's tape from the base of the petal or leaf for about 2 cm (¾ in) as this aids the petals or leaves to grip. Parafilm may be cut into two or three narrow strips, then stretched as finely as possible. When assembling, be sure that all wires are wound round the same way.

Tiger Lily

On the real flower, the stamens are fleshy, however, for decorating purposes a better result is achieved with prepared bought stamens.

Step 1: Stiffen seven long stamens and attach triangular heads of modelling fondant to six. To the seventh (the stigma) attach a tiny ball of green-coloured modelling fondant. Attach wire and bind with narrow stretched parafilm or florist's tape.

Tiger lily

Step 2: Take a ball of modelling fondant, insert moistened wire, roll and cut one petal (see pattern, page 83). Vein, ruffle and flute. Dry over a curved surface.

Step 3: Cut five more petals and shape as above. Allow to dry. Bind all petals 2.5 cm (1 in) from base with finely stretched parafilm or florist's tape.

Step 4: Pipe tiny dots on the petals using royal icing and a very fine tube. The colour of the dots match the colour of the stamen heads. Do not pipe the dots right to the tip.

Step 5: Tint petals, dots and stamen heads and allow to dry.

Step 6: Assemble three petals in a triangle; in the alternate spaces assemble the next three petals to form a second triangle. Wind all wires firmly in the same direction.

Step 7: Place stamens in position; twist the wires firmly.

Step 8: Bind all wires with stretched parafilm or florist's tape. Adjust petals if necessary.

Cymbidium

Cymbidium

Colour the modelling fondant in off-white or a pale shade of the colour you require.

Step 1: Mould a small column, insert wire, curve and allow to dry.

Step 2: Make three sepals (see pattern, page 82). Take a small piece of modelling fondant, flatten slightly and insert

This lovely wedding cake reflects a union between East and West. Decorated in the white and gold wedding colours, it takes its unusual five-sided shape from a Japanese 'good luck' symbol. The wired white bauhinias (page 48) were the bride's favourite flower

moistened wire; roll out fondant finely. Cut three sepals. Finger cut edges and vein. No. 1 is dried over a curved surface, while Nos. 2 and 3 should be dried as a pair.

Step 3: Wire, roll and cut two wing petals (4 and 5), finger cut edges and vein. Dry as a pair as illustrated.

Step 4: Cut throat, finger cut edges, vein and flute edge and add to the dried wired column.

Step 5: Pinch two fine lines (A and B) for the pollinia with tweezers while the throat is soft, or pipe two fine lines when it is dry.

Step 6: Wind a narrow strip of parafilm or florist's tape 2 cm (¾ in) down from the base of the petals, sepals and throat.

Step 7: To assemble: Take sepals 1, 2 and 3, hold firmly at base and twist wires. Add petals 4 and 5 (one on either side of No. 1 sepal), place the throat in the centre and firmly twist all wires in the one direction. Cover the wire stem with stretched parafilm or florist's tape for about 5 cm (2 in) and gently adjust petals to the required positions. Colour as desired.

Cattleya

Cattleya

Step 1: Take a piece of modelling fondant about the size of a large pea, mould a column, insert wire and dry over a curved surface.

Step 2: Take another piece of modelling fondant, flatten slightly, insert moistened wire and roll out finely. Using the pattern on page 82, cut three sepals, vein and finger cut edges. Dry No. 1 sepal with a slight curve, and Nos. 2 and 3 as a pair.

Step 3: Cut two wing petals (4 and 5) vein, flute edges from

46

A to B and dry as a pair (see pattern).

Step 4: Cut throat, finger cut edges, vein flute and add to the dry wired column. Allow to dry.

Step 5: Wind a narrow strip of parafilm or florist's tape about 2.5 cm (1 in) from the base of the petals and store.

Step 6: To assemble: Take sepals 1, 2 and 3, twist holding firmly at base. Add petals 4 and 5 (one on either side of sepal No. 1) and lastly add the throat. Wind all wires firmly in one direction. Cover the wire stem with parafilm or florist's tape for about 5 cm (2 in) and gently adjust petals to required position. Colour as desired.

Phalaenopsis

Phalaenopsis

The phalaenopsis, moth orchid or bridal orchid may be wired for convenience. The method given here is slightly different to that used for setting with royal icing when a calyx with wire is added to the back of the orchid. Both methods are worth a try and each have their place in decorating.

Step 1: Cut six pieces of wire each 7.5 cm (3 in) long.

Step 2: See pattern, page 82. Mould a tiny column, shaped like a miniature cobra's head, and allow to dry.

Step 3: Take a small ball of fondant, insert moistened wire and roll out finely. Cut out throat and place in a plastic iceball tray, curving the two sides into the hollow of the tray with the lip curving and the wire standing up.

Step 4: Cut two lobes using a tiny petal cutter, finger, curve and place into the iceball tray to dry. Remove point of petal.

Step 5: Wire and cut three sepals, finger cut edges, vein and shape tips slightly. Allow to dry on a piece of foam as this is a fairly flat flower.

Step 6: Wire and cut a pair of wing petals, finger cut edges, vein and stretch but do not flute. Allow to dry on foam also.

Step 7: Pollinia. Shape a tiny piece of modelling fondant, indenting with a knife to resemble two pieces side-by-side. Trim the back to enable it to sit flat. Allow to dry.

Step 8: Attach pollinia to throat.

Step 9: Tint all parts as required.

Step 10: To assemble: Take the column and curved throat, attach the column to the back of the throat, winding all wires firmly down in the same direction. Take the three sepals and place in position. Add the two wing petals, then attach lobes to the throat with a tiny amount of royal icing on the base of the lobe. Use tweezers for positioning. Prop up with cotton balls if necessary (if placed with care they will remain in position). Once the lobes are dry, sepals and petals may be moved to suit. Wind each wire from the base of the petal for about 2.5 cm (1 in) and cover with narrow stretched parafilm or florist's tape, then wind the wires together and cover with stretched parafilm or florist's tape.

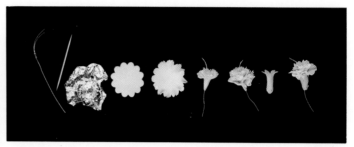

Pinks

Pinks

This is an easy method of making a pink or tiny carnation. A 5 cm (2 in) scalloped pastry cutter is a very effective and easy tool for cutting out the desired shapes.

Flower

Step 1: Roll out a piece of modelling fondant as finely as possible. Cut three shapes, covering two, while working on the one.

Step 2: With a small, sharp knife, cut a tiny slit in the base of each scallop, and three cuts on the outer curve to resemble a fringe.

Step 3: Roll a small round cocktail stick to and fro about 1 cm (½ in) in from the edge to flute. Exert the pressure on the edge of the modelling fondant.

Step 4: Brush with egg white or water, fold in halves. Brush right-hand side with egg white and fold toward the centre; brush the back of the left half and fold back (to resemble an 'S' shape). This is the centre of the flower.

Step 5: Push a hooked wire down through the middle of the centre and finger firmly on to the wire. Allow to dry.

Step 6: Repeat steps 2 and 3 with the other two shapes. Add the two moistened shapes to the centre and firm on. This should form a half-moon shaped flower, ready for a calyx to cover the surplus fondant at the base of the fluted petals.

Calyx

Step 1: Take a piece of green coloured modelling fondant about the size of a small almond, hollow out the centre and cut five shallow pointed petals. Finger the cut edges.

Step 2: Moisten the inside of calyx and sepal tips, push this up the wire to encase surplus fondant. The sepals are now attached to the underside of the flower.

Step 3: While the calyx is still soft, embed scissor points five times around the base to give the impression of a second calyx just above the stalk.

Buds

To make a bud, take one flower shape and follow Steps 2-4 for Flower; repeat Step 1 for Calyx; add 'S' shape to calyx.

Easy carnation

Easy Carnation

This carnation is shaped by placing a piece of foil over a ring of modelling fondant. The circular shapes are cut with a fluted pastry cutter. Roll out the fondant as finely as possible, otherwise the finished flower looks too heavy.

Step 1: Mould a ring of modelling fondant about 2.5 cm (1 in) in circumference, allow to dry.

Step 2: Place a piece of foil over the ring, making sure there is a hollow in the centre.

Step 3: Roll out a piece of modelling fondant finely, stamp out a circle with a fluted pastry cutter.

Step 4: With a small, sharp knife, cut a tiny slit in the base of each scallop, and three cuts on the outer curve to resemble a fringe.

Step 5: Roll a small round cocktail stick to and fro about 1 cm (¼ in) in from the edge to flute. Exert the pressure on the edge of the modelling fondant.

Step 6: Place on the foil; push down in the centre to hollow. Repeat the process several times (approximately four), adding each inside the previous layer, until the flower has a full rounded appearance. It may be necessary for the last one to be folded in an 'S' shape and pushed into the centre. Allow to dry. Attach a calyx if required.

Cyclamen

These flowers vary in size from 2.5 cm (1 in) to 7 cm (2¾ in) and may have five or six petals, which are nearly the same shape as frangipani, but with a straight edge at the base.

Buds vary in size and shape according to age. Early buds

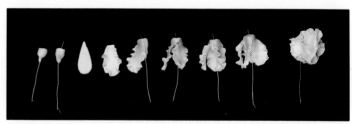

Cyclamen

are very pointed with a slight twist, while the mature bud is long and straight.

This is an unusual flower for moulding and may be used on all types of cakes. Cyclamens come in many colours, from white to pink, cerise and mauve. Their leaves make an attractive addition to the floral spray.

Step 1: Hollow out a basic cone and insert a hooked moistened wire, strong enough to support the flower. Bind with a narrow strip of parafilm at the base of the wire down about 2.5 cm (1 in). Pipe a seed capsule in the centre of the cone; depending on the variety, this may be brown, green or yellow.

Step 2: Insert several stamens. Paint a calyx on the back of the cone with thinned down royal icing. Allow to dry.

Step 3: Cut three petals using a frangipani cutter (or see pattern, page 83). Frill the edges but cut a straight edge at the base.

Step 4: Attach the petals evenly around the lip of the prepared cone. Allow to dry.

Step 5: Cut three more petals and attach in alternate spaces over the first row. Allow to dry.

Step 6: Brush colour at the base of the flower and bend the wire very gently, so that the petals are pointing upwards. Chalks are most suitable for colouring this flower.

Courtesy of Beverley Wilkinson.

Miniature dendrobium

Miniature Dendrobium

The method used to make this flower could be adapted to suit most types of orchids, including the Singapore orchid.

Step 1: Using the pattern on page 82 as a guide, cut the three sepal-shape from soft aluminium (e.g., a soft-drink can). Shape between fingers to curl the tips and give the desired effect. Use this as a mould for drying and forming the petals.

Step 2: To make the column, use a small ball of modelling paste and roll 1 cm (¼ in) long. Use ball tool to hollow the underside and open out the tip. Cut the tip into three sections. Fold side edges in and centre section down. If making as a wired flower, wire the column. Allow to dry.

Step 3: Roll out modelling paste for the throat. Cut out throat. Flute and curl the front edges.

Step 4: Roll the base of the throat around the dried column. Pull the lip down and work the top edges over the column to give an oval shape. Set aside to dry. Cotton balls give good support for drying the throat, as they help to keep the shape.

Step 5: To make the sepals, roll the modelling paste sufficiently large enough to cut the three-sepal shape. Finger cut edges finely. Vein each sepal. Place in the mould and shape the sepals carefully. The ball tool will help to work it into position. If making as a wired flower make a small hole in the centre of the shape to allow for the wire. Allow to dry.

Step 6: Cut the wing petals from rolled modelling paste. Finger the cut edges, vein and pinch along the centre of each petal. Dampen base and side of each petal as it is formed and place inside the three-sepal mould. Work carefully into place.

Step 7: To assemble: Dampen the back of the dried throat and push firmly into place inside the two wing petals while the paste is still soft. Colour when dry. Leave the flower in the mould during colouring to protect it from breakage. If making as a wired flower, pass the wire from the column through the three-sepal shape. Bind the wire with parafilm or florist's tape.

Courtesy of Pat Reay.

White Bauhinia

On the real flower, the stamens are fleshy, however, for decorating purposes, we prefer the result achieved with pre-

White bauhinia

pared bought stamens. This flower also blooms in shades of pink and mauve.

Step 1: Prepare five long, brown-tipped stamens. Tint stamen cottons green and allow to dry. Attach to fine wire with narrow parafilm. Prepare the stigma by using a white stamen with a small narrow piece of modelling fondant wrapped around the middle to represent a miniature bean or seedbox. Curve and allow to dry. Tint pale green.

Step 2: Cut five pieces of wire about 7.5 cm (3 in) long.

Step 3: Using the pattern on page 82, prepare the two wired wing petals (1 and 2) left and right. Vein, flute and ruffle edges. Place on a drying rack or slightly curved surface, such as crimpled aluminium foil or waxed paper.

Step 4: Prepare two wired lower petals (3 and 4) as in Step 3 and dry as a pair.

Step 5: Prepare a wired throat. Flute, vein and curve the base. Lay to dry with the lip overhanging. When dry, paint the base of the throat a pale green. Bind all wires with parafilm or florist's tape for about 2.5 cm (1 in) from the base of the petal.

Step 6: To assemble: Take prepared stamens and throat and hold firmly at the base, winding all wires in the one direction. Place the two lower petals on either side of the throat, add the two wing petals, one on either side of the stamen cluster, and wind down in the same way. Bind all wires with stretched parafilm or florist's tape and trim. Adjust petals gently to the required shape.

Pearls (page 55) can be combined with floral decorations to really make a cake something special. This cake features a triple flounce, as well as flowers including frangipani and small cutter flowers

VII
SPECIAL DECORATIONS

In this chapter we have included a number of decorations
and techniques which will give you additional scope in your work.

Simple piping and crimper and cutter work can be used on cakes
for less flamboyant occasions; delicate filigree piping decorations
can add that finishing touch to a stunning wedding cake; cameos and
pearls will give distinction to cakes for many various occasions.

Piping: small designs, including animals (page 52)

Simple designs for piping in royal icing

Piping

Small Designs, Including Animals

Suitable small designs for cakes are often hard to find. Here we have illustrated several attractive outlines which could be used on cakes. The step-by-step piping of animals is worth persevering with as small animal designs can look very appealing on children's cakes and Christening cakes.

Simple Designs for Piping in Royal Icing

Some people prefer a butter or sponge cake for their birthday, rather than a heavy fruit cake. These cakes require a simple decoration. A warm icing, when set, provides a suitable surface for the piped designs shown here. These can be done in royal icing in a short time and look very effective.

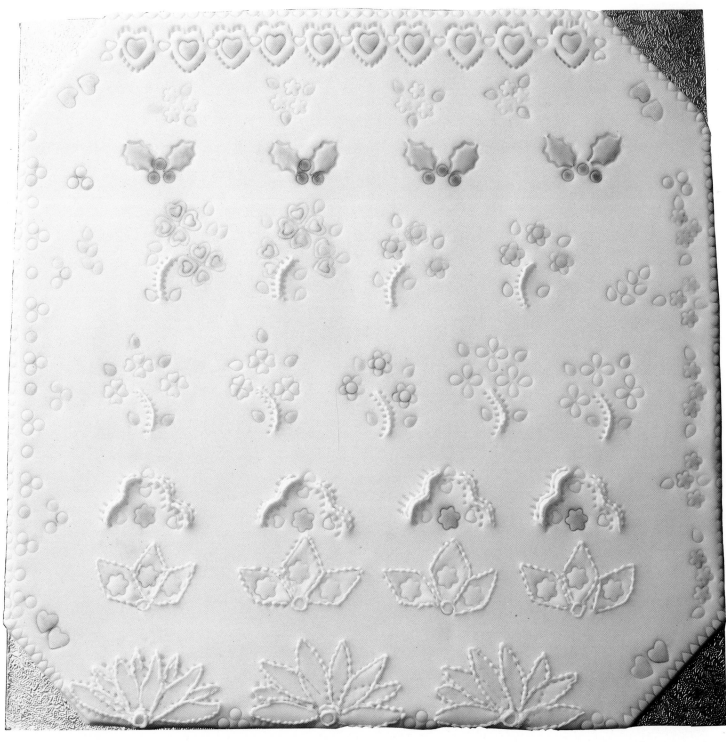

Crimper and cutter work

Crimper and Cutter Work

The decorator can create many interesting designs on all types of cakes using crimpers and cutters.

Some people prefer to use crimpers on the sides of cakes and cutters on the tops of cakes to give embroidery designs, thus eliminating pipework. The use of crimpers and cutters is quicker than pipework and is very effective. Various non-toxic coloured chalks may be dusted on the designs to give contrast with the main colour.

Filigree Piping

Finely piped filigree piping is dainty and fairylike. Bells, stars, balls, trees, a bride and groom, ring cases and slippers, are decorations which can be made in this way.

For extra strength in filigree piping, add ½ level teaspoon of gum tragacanth to a one egg white quantity of royal icing. Sprinkle the gum over the icing and beat in thoroughly. Allow to stand overnight and beat well again before commencing to pipe. Tartaric acid (⅛ teaspoon) added to royal

Filigree piping

icing also gives added strength. Royal icing for filigree piping *must* be very, very well beaten.

Special designs are available for filigree work. Also the rounded letters X, S and C, piped at random with all letters touching (see pattern, page 87), form an attractive design.

Step 1: Draw pattern and design (some patterns are given on pages 81 and 87) on to a piece of paper.

Step 2: Place this piece of paper on a board and cover with waxed paper.

Step 3: Using a No. 0 or 00 tube, pipe the design, following the drawing. All piping must link up.

Step 4: Allow to dry – leave for 24 hours. Place near gentle warmth, then very carefully remove waxed paper from piping.

Step 5: If making a decoration with more than one piece, join the pieces together with royal icing. Support with balls of cotton wool to keep the pieces in position until the joins dry.

Note: Filigree piping decorations are very fragile.

Cameos

Cameos are a versatile and attractive addition to a cake. They may be moulded, allowed to set and then decorated at a later date – this can be very handy for busy people. Alternatively both base and subject can be flooded with royal icing.

Cameos can be used as a locket (pipe the chain on to the cake and retouch it with non-toxic gold or silver paint), arranged with a string of pearls, or arranged with a spray of flowers. Here we give instructions for a floral cameo, a monogrammed cameo and a medallion cameo.

Cameo base

Roll out a piece of modelling or covering fondant thinly and cut out a small shape – oval, round or any desired shape. Allow to dry. Edges may be smoothed with a fine emery board if modelling fondant is used.

Floral Cameo

Step 1: Prepare tiny moulded flowers beforehand and allow to dry.

Step 2: Place the base shape on waxed paper. With thinned down royal icing, flood within the outline, using a fine paint brush.

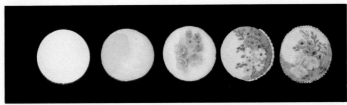

Floral cameo

Step 3: After about 30 minutes, and while the royal icing is still soft, arrange a tiny spray of flowers, pushing them into the floodwork. They should embed slightly. Allow to dry. Pipe or paint tiny leaves and stems to highlight the flowers.

Step 4: Finish the border with a simple piped edge using a No. 0 or 1 tube. Touch up with gold or silver non-toxic paint if desired.

Flooded Monogram

Step 1: Using a modelling paste base, flood and allow to dry.

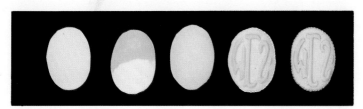

Flooded monogram

Step 2: Using a No. 000 tube and having chosen a suitable script, outline the required initials.

Step 3: Flood the outlined initials with a contrasting colour. Allow to dry. Touch up the edges of the initials with a deeper shade. Pipe a tiny border around the base to finish off.

Floodwork Medallion

Cameos can be made in one colour, or the modelling fondant base can be one colour, and the floodwork a contrasting colour.

Step 1: Flood the desired base shape and allow to dry.

Floodwork medallion

Step 2: The design of the head may be drawn or flooded freehand (see pattern, page 90). Pipe the face outline with a very fine tube. The hair is flooded with a thick royal icing; then, just before it dries, it is piped over with a No. 00 tube. The eye should be indented with a needle or pin, in line with the bridge of the nose.

The floodwork medallion described above is very attractive but it is also very fragile. Alternatively, the medallion may be shaped in modelling paste and flooded – this method is stronger.

Pearls

Pearls are another versatile decoration. They can be intertwined amongst flowers. They can be used as rosary beads, or threaded, or placed on a chain. The finished pearls are very realistic; they may be coloured as desired. The pearls are not edible.

Step 1: Roll tiny balls of modelling fondant and pierce with an embroidery needle. Allow to dry.

Step 2: Thread on to a long cotton thread, leaving a space between each pearl.

Step 3: Paint each ball with pearl nail polish and allow to dry. Move up and down the thread to prevent sticking.

Step 4: Paint the pearls over once again and leave to dry. Use as desired.

The floral cards (see text, page 59) make wonderful and
unusual decorations

VIII
MOULDED ORNAMENTS

Ornaments such as these can be a delightful addition to the apex of a cake. Although posies of flowers can be colourful, sometimes an ornament is more in keeping with the design of the cake, or the occasion for which the cake is intended. We have endeavoured to show a cross-section of ornaments to stimulate the decorator's imagination and to illustrate just what can be achieved with a good idea, a pattern and/or a mould.

'3D' plaque

'3D' Plaque

A picture may be built up in stages using modelling fondant, floodwork and painting to give depth of field. Plaques form a useful and interesting part of decorating, enabling scenes in sugar to be transferred to cakes. Gift cards or wrapping papers offer many suitable designs and ideas.

The picture has been divided into sections:
a. The *round base* of modelling fondant, onto which the sky and far-off hills and river have been flooded,
b. the *half base* of modelling fondant which has also been flooded to represent the green grass,
c. the *bridge* and *animals* are flooded on to waxed paper,
d. the *painted trees* and *bushes* are piped and flooded, and
e. the *collar* of floodwork is placed in position to form a frame for the picture.

Step 1: Roll out a piece of modelling fondant very finely and cut to the desired shape (see pattern, page 89). Allow to dry. Smooth any rough edges carefully with emery paper. Trace the sky, far-off hills and the river on this shape. When the shape has dried well, flood in the sky, hills and river with thinned-down royal icing.

'3D' plaque

Step 2: Cut a second shape to represent the green grass (see pattern, page 89). Flood in green.

Step 3: Place a piece of waxed paper over the selected designs, and using royal icing and a No. 0 tube outline the two pieces of the bridge and all animals. Flood in suitable colours. Allow to dry. Paint in details. Remove carefully from paper when dry.

Step 4: Make more than one collar in case one breaks on removing from the paper. Position the pattern for the collar under glass or clear perspex to keep it firm; place waxed paper on top of the glass and secure. Using a No. 1 tube and royal icing, pipe the collar outline onto the paper and allow to dry for a short time. Flood with thinned-down royal icing, working around the collar in both directions to complete the circle. This method of joining moist floodwork eliminates a join in the crusted royal icing. Allow to dry thoroughly – this

may take several days. Remove the waxed paper with extreme care – place the collar on a turntable or near a table edge and gently pull the paper with a downward movement.

When flooding a large area, use actiwhite powder or freeze-dried albumen in the royal icing (see recipe, page 69) for best results. Egg white may not dry out satisfactorily.

Step 5: To assemble: position the round base in the centre of a covered board or cake and secure with a little royal icing. Add cut-out green grass section, using a little royal icing to secure.

Add the bridge, trees and animals in the foreground. Retouch any small details with a fine paint brush if necessary.

Pipe an edging all round the collar and allow to dry. Pipe a shell about 1 cm (½ in) around the extreme edge of the completed plaque and carefully position the collar to form a frame for the scene.

The Floral Card

Inspiration for this decoration can be gained from the many cards available. Florists sometimes use a card and fresh flowers to make a special arrangement. The card can be made in sugar and may be kept as a memento.

Step 1: Roll out a piece of modelling fondant *very* finely and cut out a suitable size. Our model is 15 x 10 cm (6 x 4 in) approximately (see pattern, page 91).

Step 2: Cut a circle or oval in the centre of the card and punch two small holes on the left-hand side for the ribbon, which holds the card together. While soft, press a fancy-tipped souvenir spoon around the cut edges, using a little cornflour to prevent it sticking.

Step 3: Cut another piece for the back of the card and punch two corresponding holes to match the front piece. (Do not cut a hole in the centre of this piece.) Allow to dry.

Step 4: Mould suitable flowers and leaves, using slightly longer wires. Allow to dry and tint as desired.

Step 5: Insert ribbon through the holes and finish with a flat bow in the front. Set the card in a half-open standing position. Place a small ball of covering fondant as a foundation for the spray, behind the centre front. Secure with a little royal icing. Allow to dry.

Step 6: Place the base of the spray into the ball of covering fondant foundation from the outside, through the cut shape. To hide any of the foundation which may be showing, insert ribbon loops and small flowers and buds.

'3M' plaque

'3M' Plaque

This plaque was made using three methods: the moulding of flowers, brush embroidery and the painting of ferns and small leaves. It makes a very attractive feature for the top of a cake. The combined use of the three methods gives a lift to the finished article. Designs may be traced from embroidery patterns. See our patterns, pages 90 and 91.

Step 1: Roll out a piece of modelling fondant as finely as possible to the desired shape and size. Imprint the edge with the tip of a souvenir spoon, or any type of suitable fancy edging. Allow to dry. Smooth any rough edges with emery paper. Spray or chalk a delicate colour if desired.

Step 2: Pipe the basic outline of the spray with royal icing.

Step 3: Brush embroider the leaves, buds and calyx, also the butterfly.

Step 4: Using a fine paint brush (No. 00) paint on the fern, using diluted food colouring (it would be too dark if painted straight from the bottle).

Step 5: Retouch the edge of the plaque with silver or gold non-toxic paint.

Step 6: Arrange a few small moulded briar roses to complete the plaque.

Brush embroidery was commenced in Australia many years ago and our American friend Joan McDaniel has been promoting this method for quite some time. Brush embroidery is very popular on wedding cakes and can be particularly useful when the bride has requested that the lace design on her frock match the lace design on the cake.

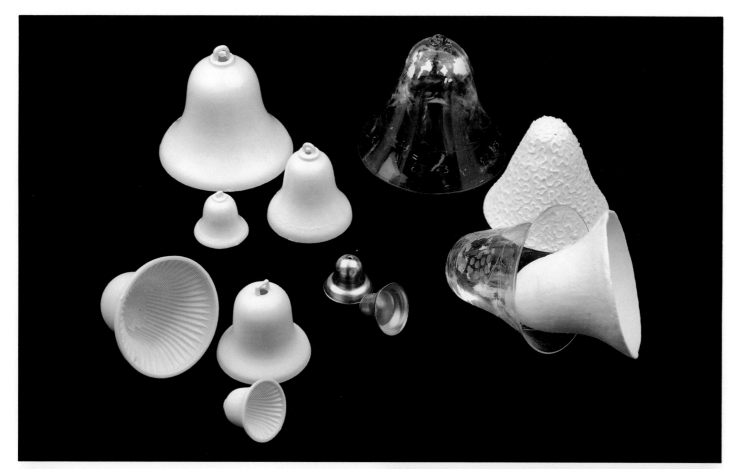

Bells

Half bells, full bells, large, small and medium-sized bells make lovely decorations, particularly for wedding cakes. Small bells may be cut in halves and placed as a pair on the sides of a wedding cake, together with soft embroidery and pearl stamens. Very small ones may be tied in groups of three and placed on the cake – remember to cut slots for the thread when moulding.

Bells can be made in two ways: but cutting out a pattern, or by pressing a ball of modelling fondant into a mould.

Large bells may have fancy rims, such as slots for threading ribbon or picot edgings; these should be cut while the bell is soft. Allow to dry thoroughly before removing from the mould and decorating.

Method 1
Step 1: Wipe the mould with a soft cloth and dust freely without cornflour.

Step 2: Take a piece of modelling fondant large enough to cover the mould; roll out and cut to the pattern (see page 87).

Step 3: Join the two straight edges of the bell, moistening with water and easing gently into the shape of the mould. Care must be taken to press the bell gently, as otherwise it could stick to the mould. While it is still soft, turn it out to make sure it is free, then return it to the mould to set.

Step 4: Camouflage the seam with flowers, ribbons, etc., held in place with covering fondant. The outside of the bell may be covered with cornelli or embroidery or left plain. The edges are finished with piped lace, a dainty shell border or pearl stamens attached with royal icing.

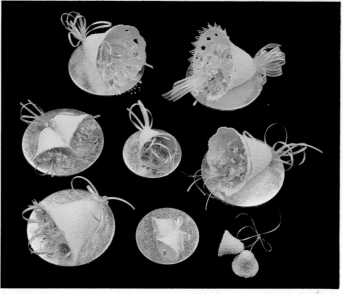

Bells

Method 2
Step 1: Wipe the mould with a soft cloth and dust freely with cornflour.

Step 2: Take a piece of modelling fondant, about the size of the diameter of the top of the bell, and thick enough to carefully spread to the rim. Use cornflour on fingertips to smooth out the shape. Taper the edge of the bell as finely as possible. It is best to remove the bell several times during the process to ensure that it does not stick to the mould. Cut along the edge with a sharp knife or scalpel and leave in the mould to dry.

Step 3: Decorate in the same way as for Method 1.

Slipper

Make a permanent pattern for future use. Select a suitable mould and, if necessary, cut along the seam to make two halves. Dust the mould with cornflour. Roll out a piece of modelling fondant very finely and press into the clean mould. Remove fondant from the mould, flatten gently and cut around the slipper shape. Allow to dry. Trace the shape on to a piece of thin cardboard, thus giving a permanent pattern.

Step 1: Roll the fondant out as finely as possible, using the pattern. Cut a shape and ease it carefully into the mould. Repeat the process, reversing the pattern to make the second half of a slipper. Allow to dry.

Step 2: Remove from the mould and using a soft brush, dust the half slipper. Gently rub down all cut edges with emery paper, and smooth any blemishes. Repeat the process for the other half.

Step 3: Join the two halves together, fill the heel with royal icing for added strength. Cover all seams with icing on the *inside* of the shoe. Scrape away any excess on the outside. Allow to dry.

Step 4: Thin down a small quantity of royal icing and, using a No. 3 paintbrush, paint all over the slipper. Stand on waxed paper to dry.

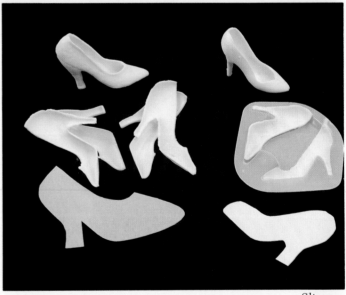

Slipper

Step 5: With royal icing, embroider or pipe cornelli work all over the slipper, using a fine tube. Embroider a small buckle by piping a circle in the centre of the shoe upper and stud it with small pearl stamens while the icing is soft.

Step 6: To decorate: place a small piece of covering fondant inside the slipper and allow to firm overnight. Fill with a selection of small flowers and ribbon loops.

Curved shells

Curved Shells

Step 1: Collect your own shell from the beach to use as a mould. Wash and dry thoroughly and dust with cornflour.

Step 2: Roll out a piece of modelling fondant and press into the shell, using the shell as a pattern. Run your fingers around the edge of the shell and ease off the surplus.

Step 3: If you are using a very flat shell, loosen the modelling fondant and dry it out over the back of a round-bottomed patty pan. Fondant for curved shells can be dried in the shell.

Step 4: Repeat Steps 2 and 3 to make the second half of the shell.

Step 5: When dry, join the two halves at the base with a small amount of royal icing and support at the angle required until the join is dry.

Step 6: Place a small ball of covering fondant as a foundation on the bottom of the shell, and secure the fondant with a spot of royal icing.

Step 7: Cover the foundation with a selection of small flowers and ribbon loops.

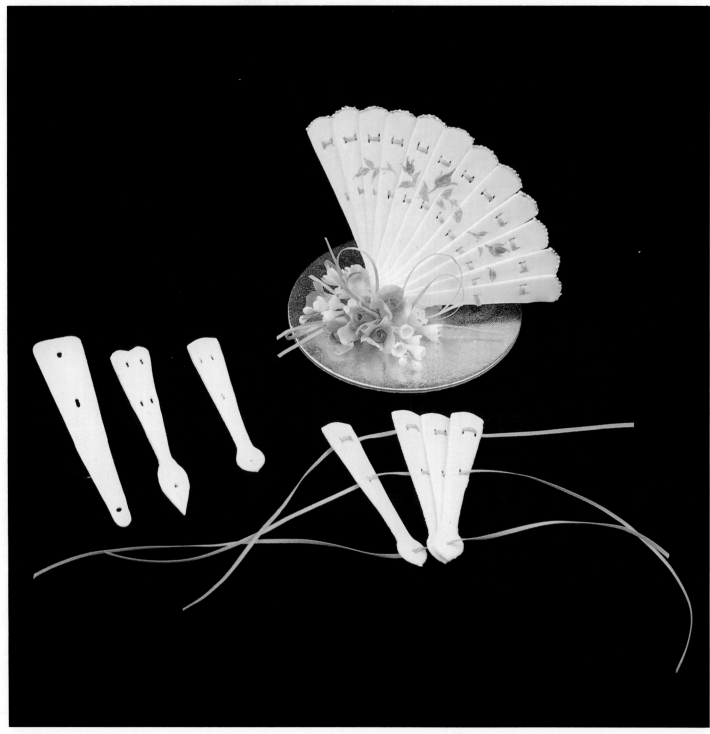

Fan

Fan

Fan cutters are available in specialist stores, however you can cut your own patterns (see page 91). Use firm cardboard for the pattern.

Step 1: Roll out fondant as finely as possible, otherwise the base becomes too bulky and the fan will lose its daintiness.

Step 2: Cut out approximately 15-16 slats to complete the fan. First decide on the width of the ribbon to be used, then cut slots carefully and cleanly. If there are any rough edges it is very hard to thread the ribbon through it. Allow to dry.

Step 3: Thread ribbon carefully through the slots and secure at the back with a spot of royal icing. Each slat overlaps at the top slightly. Secure at the base with a spot of royal icing between each slat. Allow to dry. Place a short pearl-headed stamen in the hole.

Step 4: Flowers used for this display should be tiny. Use the flower of your choice and ribbon loops to soften the arrangement. The fan may be displayed flat on the cake, or supported back and front with flowers.

Vase

Vase

A simple vase can be made by rolling out a piece of modelling fondant as finely as possible, cutting it to a pattern (see page 90), draping it over a cream horn mould, and allowing it to set. The seam must be kept as neat as possible.

Step 1: The base is a small disc. Cut it with a fluted cutter (a bottletop would be suitable). Allow it to dry in the base of an egg cup or curved patty pan.

Step 2: When dry, sandpaper the seam and both edges. Attach the point of the cone to the centre of the curved disc. Support with cotton balls to dry.

Step 3: Embroider or pipe cornelli work all over and neaten the top edge with a small snail's trail. Allow to dry.

Step 4: Fill with small flowers. The vase may be coloured or touched up with gold or silver non-toxic paint.
A Grecian urn may be made by using a large bell mould for the top and a smaller bell mould for the base. Join the two domes and embroider in the same way.

Choir boys or angels

Choir Boys or Angels

The Christmas theme often calls for choir boys or angels on a cake or as a table decoration. This method of moulding with modelling fondant is great fun for all – and simple to do. Choir boys and angels may also be made from covering fondant or a mixture of both.

Step 1: Mould a conical shape 4 cm (1½ in) high in red-coloured modelling fondant or a mixture of modelling and covering fondants. Attach tiny arms and curve to the front. Allow to dry.

Step 2: Roll out a piece of white covering fondant and cut out a round with a 5 cm (2 in) fluted cutter. Flounce the edges. This is now the surplice.

Step 3: Drape the surplice over the arms and body, making the back slightly longer than the front, leaving space in the sleeve for the hands to be inserted.

Step 4: Cut two smaller rounds, 2.5 cm (1 in) in red and 2 cm (¾ in) in white for the collars. Flute and place on top of the surplice.

Step 5: Mould a small head tinted pink and allow to dry. Paint the face and hair using a fine paintbrush, and allow to dry. Place in position with a spot of royal icing.

Step 6: Mould the clasped hands and place in position with a little royal icing.

Step 7: Roll out a tiny piece of fondant and shape as for a half-open book. When dry scribble a few lines to represent music. Attach with a little royal icing on top of the hands.

Step 8: Mould small brown pieces to represent the tips of shoes. Moisten and place in position.

Angels can be made in the same way, keeping the theme all white. They look very attractive if given a tiny knob of hair on the top of their head, and a small halo of gold. Wings may be made of rice paper, or very finely rolled fondant allowed to dry before placing in position.

Blushing bride

Blushing Bride

This is a dainty South African flower that contrasts in shape with other more rounded flowers. It makes an interesting addition to a spray. The flower can be made in various sizes. Although the flower is naturally a pale pink, vary the colour as desired.

Step 1: Mould a conical shaped bud on wire and allow to dry.

Step 2: Using a small sepal cutter, stamp out four shapes (see pattern, page 88). Cover the remaining three while working on one.

Step 3: Make small slits on each side of the sepal points.

Step 4: Using a ball-end tool, cup the sepal as shown. Moisten the base and attach to the bud on the wire by threading the sepal onto the wire with the tiny petals pointing towards the tip.

Step 5: Take a second shape and repeat Steps 3 and 4, sliding it onto the wire and positioning it with the petals in the alternate spaces.

Step 6: Curve the next two shapes with the ball-end tool, but do not cut. Attach each in the same way, using a little water and arrange in alternate spaces. Allow to dry.

Step 7: Tint or spray the tips with pale pink vegetable colouring.

*Nylon tulle handkerchief (page 38) combined with jasmine
and ribbon loops makes a simple but effective decoration*

IX
RECIPES AND HANDY HINTS

Royal Icing

Royal icing is a piping icing. It should be made carefully, so take time to mix it well. Buy your pure icing sugar from a busy supermarket to ensure its freshness – squeeze or shake the box before purchasing as a double check. Allow the egg to come to room temperature before using. Then separate the white, making sure none of the yolk is included. Be sure all utensils and the wooden spoon are free from all grease, as this can ruin the icing.

1 egg white
¼ teaspoon liquid glucose (optional)
250 g (8 oz) pure icing sugar
2 or 3 drops acetic acid

Beat egg white and liquid glucose lightly in a glass bowl with a wooden spoon. Add finely sieved icing sugar a tablespoon at a time, beating well between each addition until the mixture is thick and creamy. Add acetic acid and beat until blended. The icing should form and hold a smooth peak when pulled away from the mixture. (Beating time is approximately 20 minutes.) Keep in an airtight container, or cover with a damp cloth or plastic film to prevent crusting.

Actiwhite Royal Icing

30 g (1 oz) actiwhite powder
150 ml (6 fl oz) water
1.25 kg (2½ lb) pure icing sugar

Actiwhite powder is available from health-food stores. Soak powder in water for 15 minutes and sieve through muslin or a fine sieve. Add icing sugar slowly and beat for 6 minutes at full speed, 15 minutes at half speed, until the mixture becomes very thick. Store in a refrigerator and re-beat before use. Use water to correct the consistency.

Before use, work the air bubbles out of the royal icing and beat it until it is shiny and smooth. For small quantities egg white is suitable, however work out the air bubbles by using a spatula on a flat surface. Draw a pencil line and run a small quantity of icing over the line – if it covers the line, it is ready for use.

For large areas, have several plastic sandwich bags filled with the icing ready and snip the corner just before commencing to flood.

Net Stiffener

Cotton net (see Chapter I) needs to be stiffened so that it will retain the desired shape for the decoration. This mixture gives good results. If stored in the refrigerator, the mixture will keep for several months.

¾ cup pure icing sugar
½ cup cold water

Dissolve the icing sugar in the cold water and bring it slowly to the boil. Simmer gently for 10 minutes, cool and bottle.

Marzipan

This marzipan recipe is recommended for moulding the many figures described in Chapter IV. You can develop your own ideas for moulded decorations with a litle practice.

250 g (8 oz) glucose
1.5 kg (3 lb) prepared commercial marzipan
1 kg (2 lb) pure icing sugar

Soften glucose over hot water using a double saucepan. Blend with marzipan, stirring to a smooth paste. Add icing sugar gradually, kneading until the dough is firm and pliable. Colour as desired.

Modelling Fondant

Modelling fondant is used for moulded flowers, leaves, ornaments, Christmas decorations, wedding bells, bowls, etc. Follow the recipe carefully as correct consistency is of prime importance, especially for fine petals.

30 ml (1 fl oz) cold water
2 teaspoons gelatine
1 teaspoon liquid glucose
160 g (5 oz) pure sifted icing sugar
Extra sifted icing sugar

Place water in double enamel saucepan, add gelatine and stir over low heat until dissolved (do not boil); add glucose and stir until dissolved. Allow to cool, but not to become cold. Add 160 g (5 oz) sieved pure icing sugar, stirring until it is absorbed. Place in an airtight container and leave for 24 hours. The mixture should be firm and spongy when set.

When ready to commence modelling, take a small quantity of the mixture and knead extra sifted icing sugar into it, until it is of a similar consistency to plasticine. Modelling fondant keeps for longer periods if this method is used.

Flower Paste

Used worldwide, this recipe is particularly suitable for making fine petals, cut from the thinly rolled paste.

500 g (1 lb) pure icing sugar
3 teaspoons gum tragacanth
2 teaspoons gelatine
5 teaspoons cold water
2 teaspoons copha or white vegetable shortening
2 teaspoons liquid glucose
white of 1 x 55 g egg, string removed.

Lightly grease 2 basins with extra copha. Place half the sugar in each basin. Add the gum tragacanth to the sugar in one basin; cover with a clean dry tea-towel and a plate, and place over boiling water in a saucepan. Heat over low heat until the sugar is hot to the touch.

Meanwhile, place the cold water in a small metal container (such as a clean baked beans tin) and sprinkle gelatine over the surface. Let stand until the gelatine becomes spongy. Dissolve over hot (*not boiling*) water until it becomes completely clear. Only stir from time to time to prevent a skin from forming. When the gelatine is clear, add the copha and the liquid glucose; dissolve these too.

Add the dissolved gelatine mixture and the egg white to the sugar in the bowl on the stove. Keep the basin over the hot water on the stove. Use a metal spoon. Add quickly before stirring, then stir briskly until the mixture turns from a dingy beige to a good white. This takes quite a long time. Make sure that the saucepan does not boil dry. When this mixture is quite white, add it to the sugar in the second basin, stirring until it becomes too stiff to stir easily. Dispense with the spoon. Wash, dry and lightly grease hands, and knead until all the sugar is incorporated. Pull the paste as for toffee, until it is very white and pliable. Place in a clean plastic bag in an airtight container in the fridge. Store for 24 hours before use.

Recipe courtesy Denise Fryer (South Africa) and Tombi Peck

Gum Paste

Gum paste is used for single shapes that can be modelled quickly, e.g., small animals on a log cake. It is not recommended for flowers.

500 g (1 lb) pure icing sugar
2 teaspoons gelatine
¼ cup boiling water

Sift icing sugar, thoroughly dissolve gelatine in boiling water, add to half the quantity of icing sugar in a large bowl. Knead well, adding more icing sugar until the mixture is no longer sticky. Keep in a plastic bag in an airtight container.

Modelling Paste

This modelling paste is also made with extra gum tragacanth for added strength.

1 tablespoon liquid glucose
1 heaped dessertspoon gum tragacanth
½ level tablespoon gelatine
60 ml (2 fl oz) cold water
Approximately 500 g (1 lb) pure sifted icing sugar

Place all ingredients except the icing sugar in a double saucepan (enamel) and heat until quite hot (*do not boil*). Pour into a well of icing sugar and combine (you may have a little icing sugar over). Knead to a smooth consistency and place in a plastic bag in an airtight container. Stand for 48 hours before use. Use cornflour sparingly when modelling with this paste.

Pastillage

Pastillage, a mixture of royal icing and powdered gum tragacanth, is used for modelling where strength is required, for instance, for houses, churches, etc. Pastillage sets firmly in most weather. Chemists stock powdered gum tragacanth, however it may have to be ordered in advance. Sprinkle half a teaspoon of powdered gum tragacanth into a cup of well-worked royal icing and beat thoroughly with a knife. Place in an airtight container, allow to stand for 24 hours. Take desired quantity from the container, and add enough pure icing sugar to form a pliable dough (like plasticine). Knead well. Do not store in the refrigerator. Store in a plastic bag in an airtight container.

Handy Hints

- A safe way to carry liquid colours is to buy an artist's palette (a children's toy one will do) and paint a variety of colours straight from the bottle on to the palette. Allow to dry. Dilute colours as required.
- A quick and easy way to make baby's breath is to place some desiccated coconut in a blender for a short time. Dip a piece of wire in egg white and then in the coconut. Allow to dry.
- You can add subtle colour to a flower, by putting a touch of chalk on your fingers before moulding the petals. Do the same for a calyx.
- After small flowers have been cut, place them on a piece of foam rubber and shape with a ball-end tool.
- Use small cutter flowers and/or a pastry wheel to neaten the top edge of a fondant flounce.
- A coating made from 30 g (1 oz) gum arabic in ¼ cup water (dissolved in a double saucepan over boiling water) will make leaves or berries glossy.
- Tiered wedding cakes should come to an apex for good balance.
- Special sepal cutters are now available. They provide a quick and easy way to make sepals. Or you can make your own pattern using shim brass (gauge 0.005). Our pattern on page 67 for Blushsing Bride could be used.
- Work on a large piece of foam when assembling cakes as this eliminates breakages.
- Make your own stamens from left-over cottons by dipping them in egg white and then in a suitable coloured chalk.
- Make tiny buds by dipping stamens heads into thinned-down royal icing. If a larger bud is required dip them again.
- Stamens cottons may be dipped into thinned-down icing for very small stamen tips.
- Potato flour may be used in place of cornflour. Some decorators prefer its texture.
- Ribbons, stamens, and cotton net can be stiffened with sugar syrup, nail polish, clear varnish, spray starch or hairspray. These are only aids for stiffening and are obviously not edible.
- Keep the tip of your knife or scalpel damp when cutting shapes out in modelling fondant, as this helps to make a clean cut.
- If gum tragacanth is not readily available, substitute carboxymethylcellulose which is available from pharmacies.
- For really red roses, dissolve red powder with gelatine, glucose and water mixture when making modelling fondant. Then make up in the usual way. You can use half and keep the rest of the spongy mixture in the freezer. It will keep indefinitely in the freezer. This way you can have red roses without having to paint them.
- To prevent royal icing from oozing out of the bag, twist a rubber band firmly around the top.
- One teaspoon of gelatine dissolved in warm water makes an excellent 'glue' when covering boards.

STEP-BY-STEP
PHOTOGRAPHS

Rose and leaf
(*see text, page 31*)

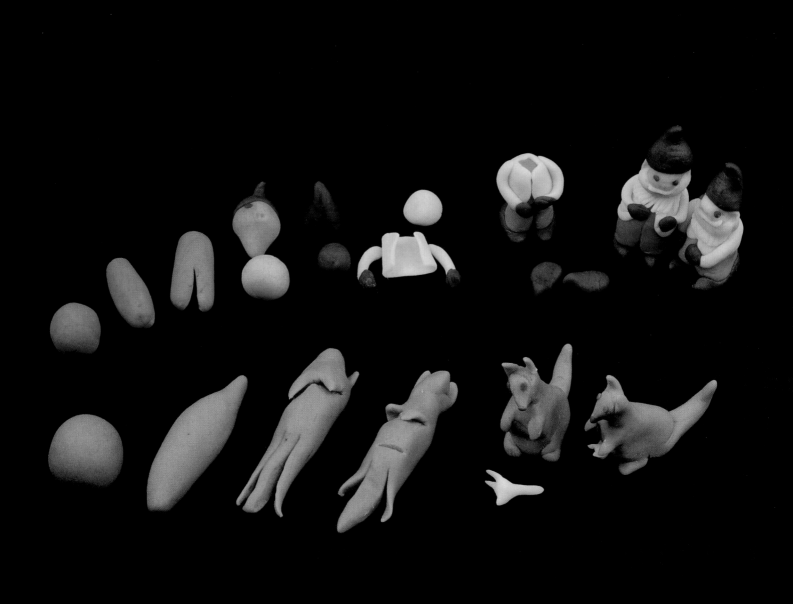

Kangaroo and Joey
(see text, page 32)

Gnome
(see text, page 35)

72

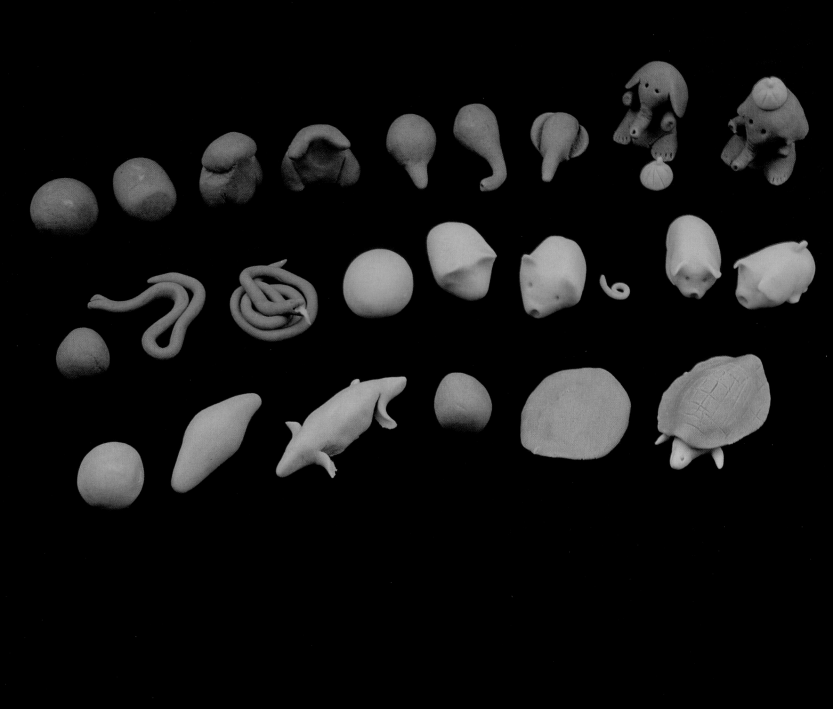

Elephant
(see text, page 32)

Snake
(see text, page 32)

Pig
(see text, page 33)

Tortoise
(see text, page 32)

Mouse
(see text, page 33)

Snail
(see text, page 33)

Duck
(see text, page 33)

Frog
(see text, page 33)

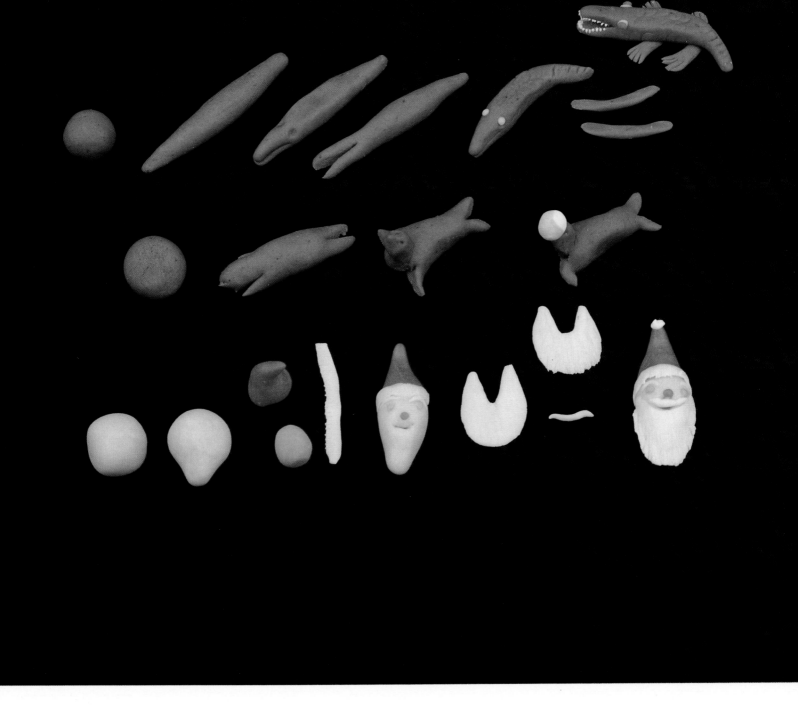

Alligator or Crocodile
(see text, page 34)

Seal
(see text, page 34)

Father Christmas Head
(see text, page 34)

Cattleya
(see text, page 46)

Tiger Lily
(see text, page 45)

Cymbidium
(see text, page 45)

Phalaenopsis
(see text, page 47)

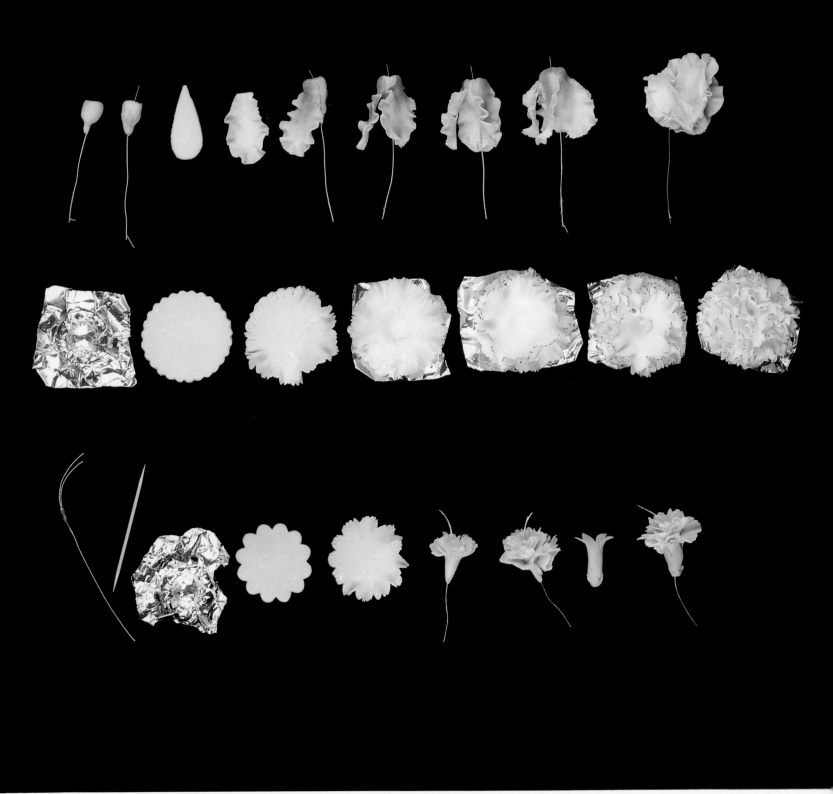

Cyclamen
(see text, page 48)

Easy Carnation
(see text, page 48)

Pinks
(see text, page 47)

Miniature Dendrobium
(see text, page 48)

White Bauhinia
(see text, page 49)

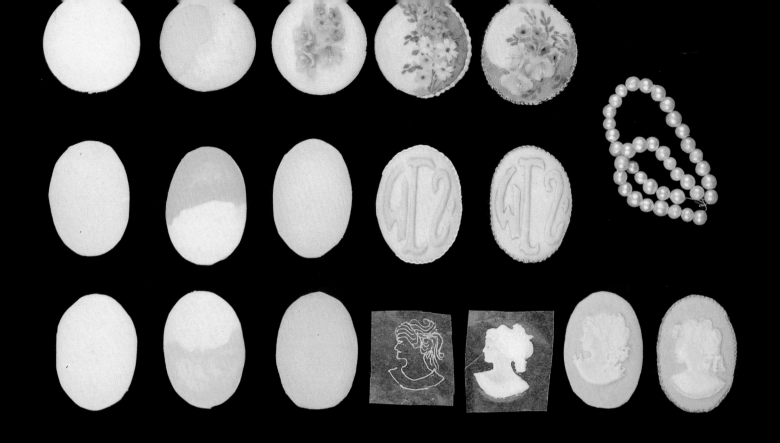

Floral Cameo
(see text, page 55)

Flooded Monogram
(see text, page 55)

Floodwork Medallion
(see text, page 55)

PATTERNS

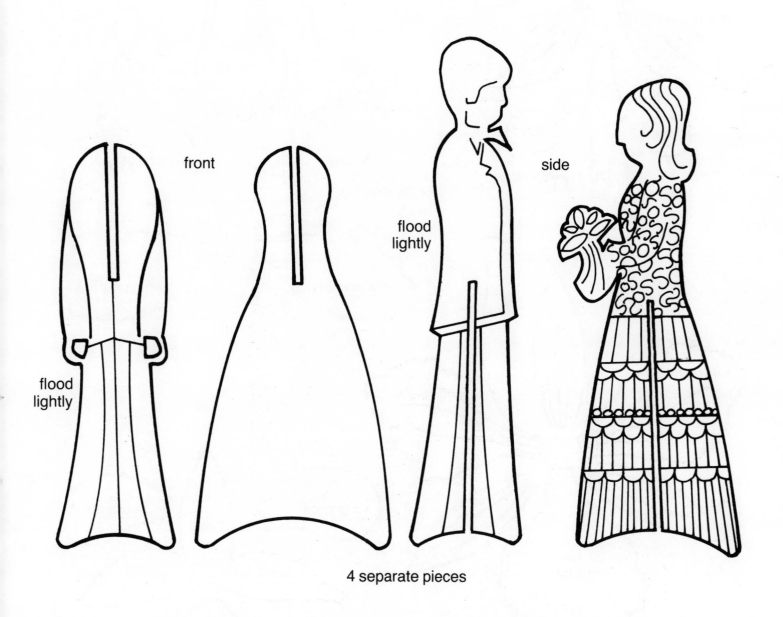

front

side

flood
lightly

flood
lightly

4 separate pieces

Bride and Groom
(filigree piping ornament, see text, page 54)

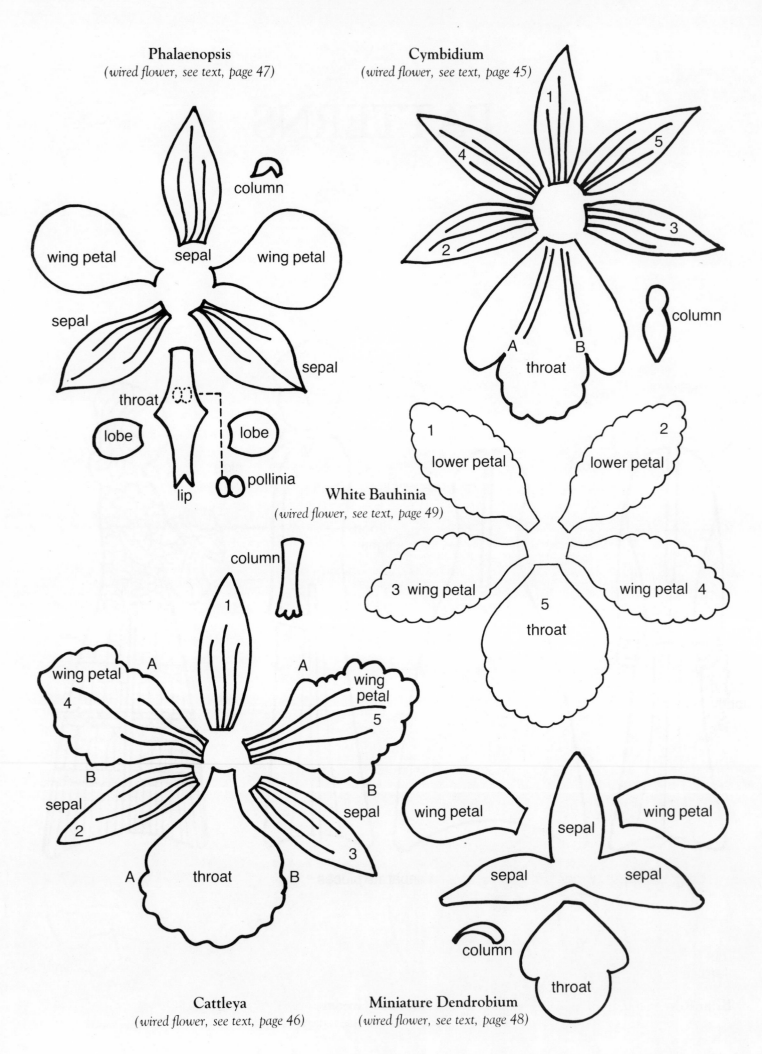

Phalaenopsis
(wired flower, see text, page 47)

column

wing petal

sepal

wing petal

sepal

sepal

throat

lobe

lobe

pollinia

lip

Cymbidium
(wired flower, see text, page 45)

1

4

5

2

3

column

A

B

throat

White Bauhinia
(wired flower, see text, page 49)

1

lower petal

2

lower petal

3 wing petal

wing petal 4

5

throat

column

1

Cattleya
(wired flower, see text, page 46)

wing petal

A

A

wing petal

4

5

B

B

sepal

sepal

2

3

A throat B

Miniature Dendrobium
(wired flower, see text, page 48)

wing petal

sepal

wing petal

sepal

sepal

column

throat

Cyclamen
(wired flower, see text, page 48)

Tiger Lily
(wired flower, see text, page 45)

Ivy Leaves
(wired leaves, see text, page 45)

Geranium/Pelargonium Leaf
(wired leaves, see text, page 45)

Maple Leaf
(wired leaves, see text, page 45)

Holly Leaf
(wired leaf, see text, page 45)

large

small

Rose Leaves
(wired leaves, see text, page 45)

Chrysanthemum Leaf
(wired leaf, see text, page 45)

Ivy Leaves
(nylon tulle leaf, see text, page 41)

cut 5
small

cut 5
large

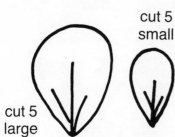

Briar Rose and Christening Rose
(cotton net flower, see text, page 15)

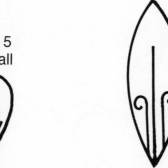

Tiger Lily
(cotton net flower, see text, page 13)

cut 9 of each
waterlily leaf

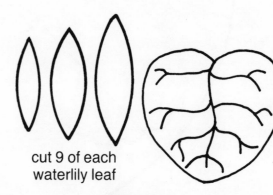

Waterlily
(cotton net flower, see text, page 14)

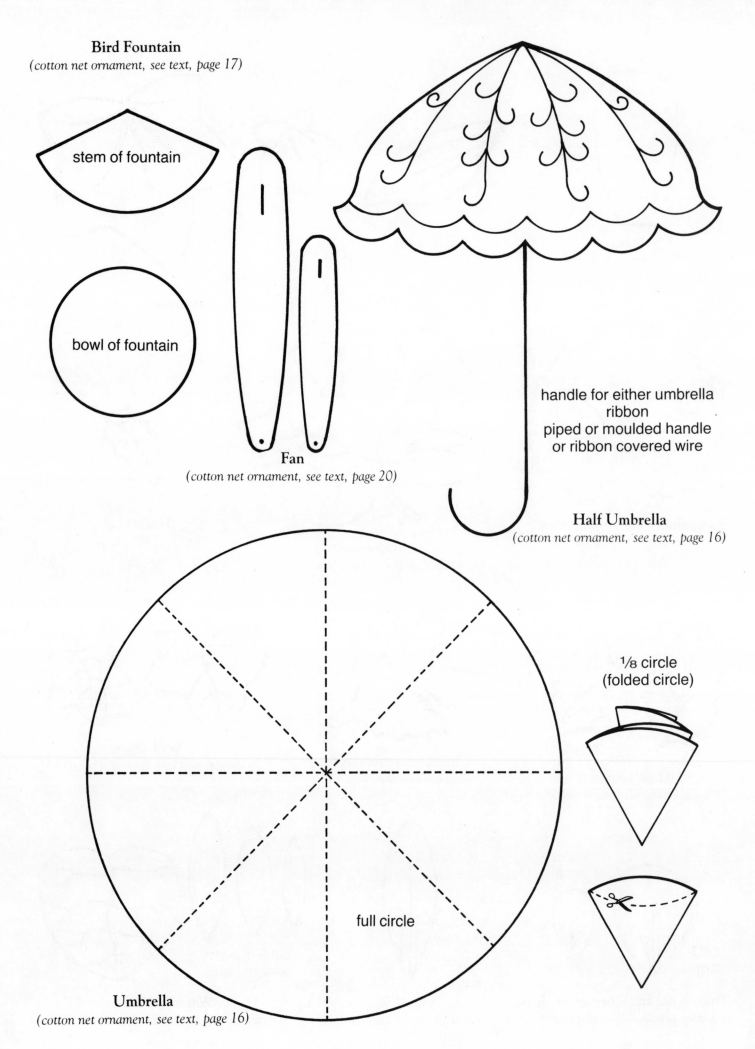

Bird Fountain
(cotton net ornament, see text, page 17)

stem of fountain

bowl of fountain

Fan
(cotton net ornament, see text, page 20)

handle for either umbrella
ribbon
piped or moulded handle
or ribbon covered wire

Half Umbrella
(cotton net ornament, see text, page 16)

⅛ circle
(folded circle)

full circle

Umbrella
(cotton net ornament, see text, page 16)

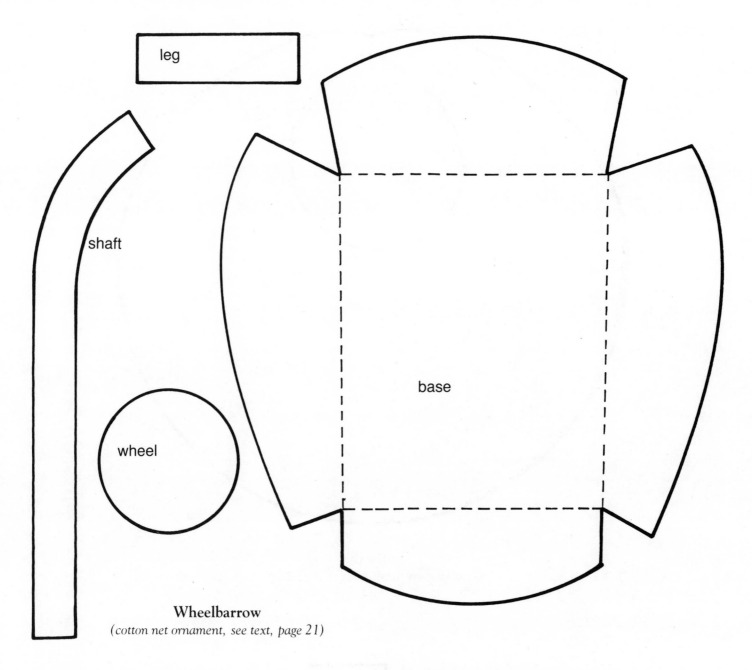

Wheelbarrow
(cotton net ornament, see text, page 21)

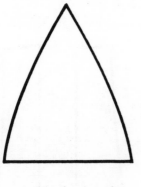

net skirt for border

Border
(cotton net ornament, see text, page 12)

Net Basket
(cotton net ornament, see text, page 19)

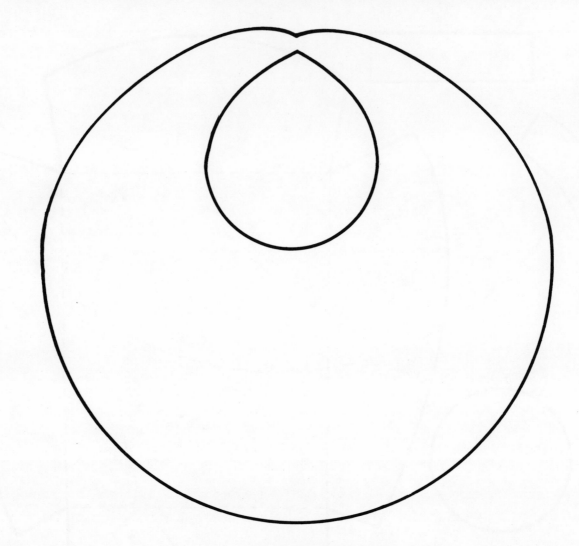

Frilled Bib
(fondant ornament, see text, page 25)

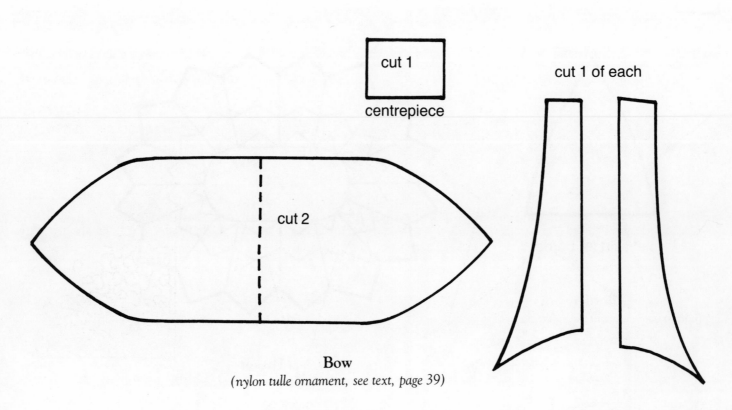

cut 1

centrepiece

cut 1 of each

cut 2

Bow
(nylon tulle ornament, see text, page 39)

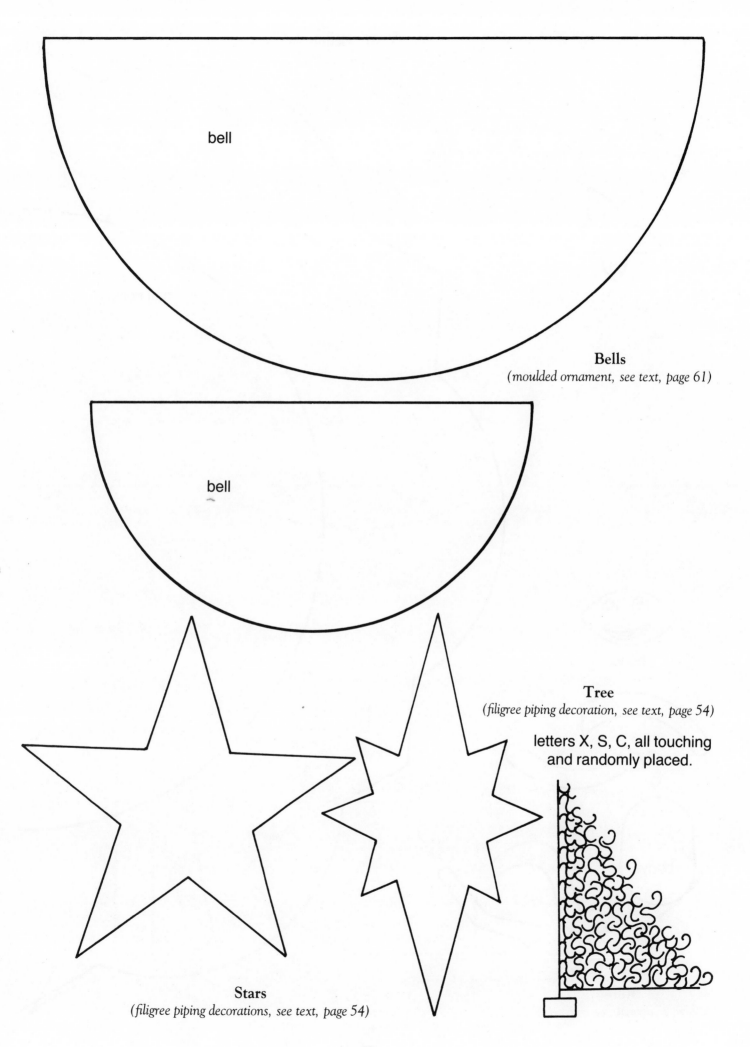

bell

Bells
(moulded ornament, see text, page 61)

bell

Tree
(filigree piping decoration, see text, page 54)

letters X, S, C, all touching
and randomly placed.

Stars
(filigree piping decorations, see text, page 54)

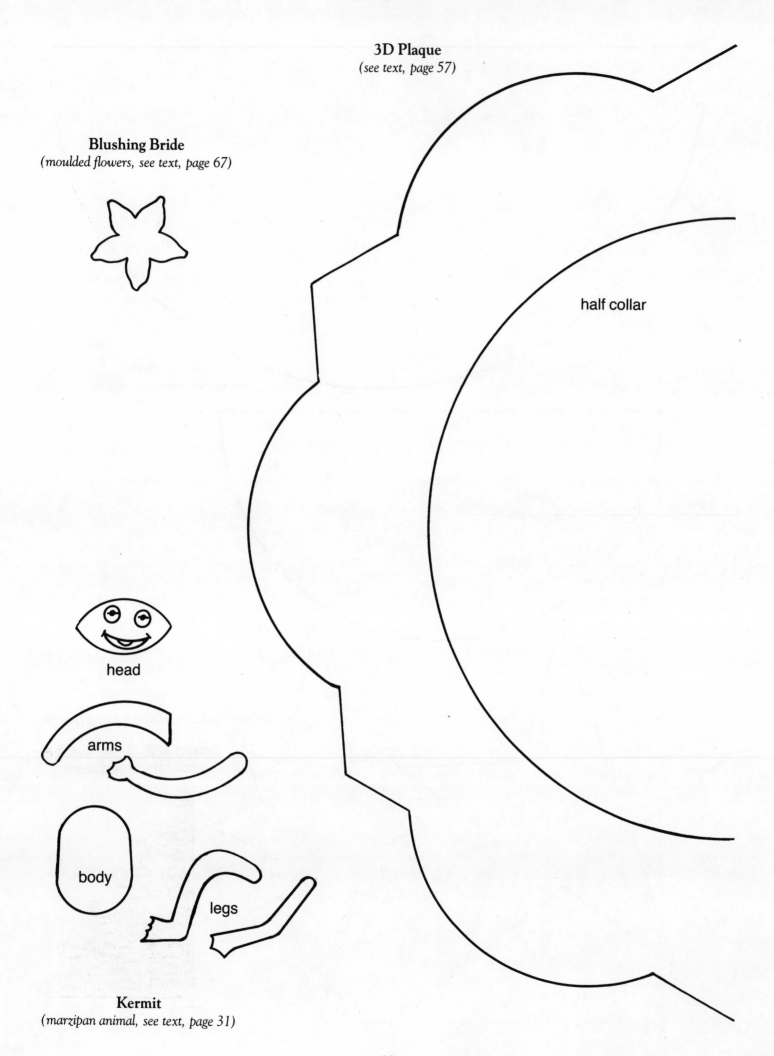

3D Plaque
(see text, page 57)

Blushing Bride
(moulded flowers, see text, page 67)

half collar

head

arms

body

legs

Kermit
(marzipan animal, see text, page 31)

88

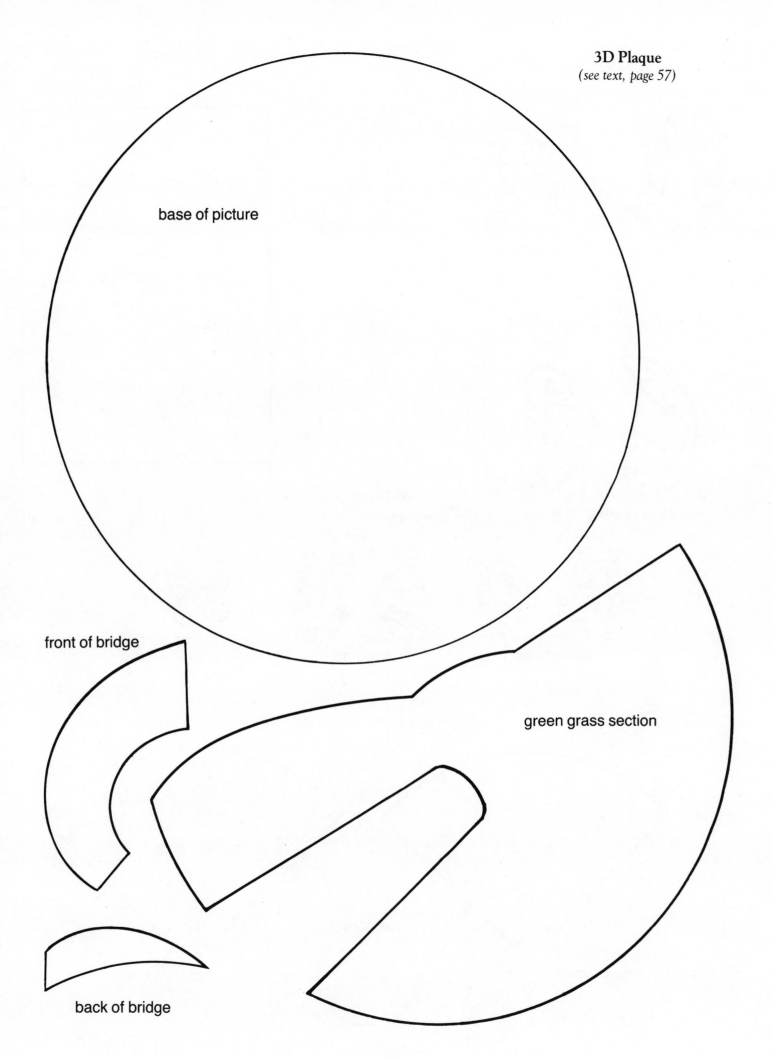

3D Plaque
(*see text, page 57*)

base of picture

front of bridge

green grass section

back of bridge

Cameo
(flooded ornament, page 55)

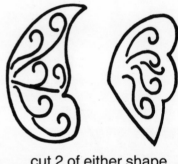

Dress
(nylon tulle, see text, page 38)

neck hole

top of dress

Butterfly
(nylon tulle ornament, see text, page 41)

cut 2 of either shape

3M Plaque
(see text, page 60)

butterfly no. 1

butterfly no. 2

Vase
(moulded ornament, see text, page 65)

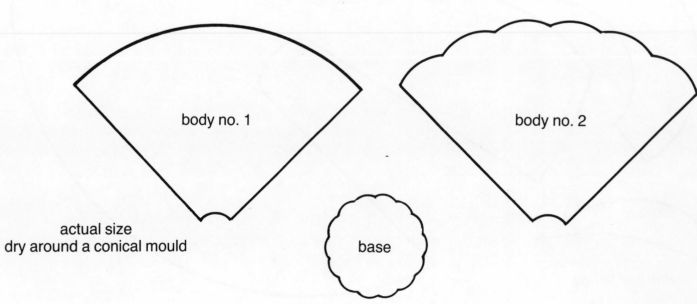

body no. 1

body no. 2

base

actual size
dry around a conical mould

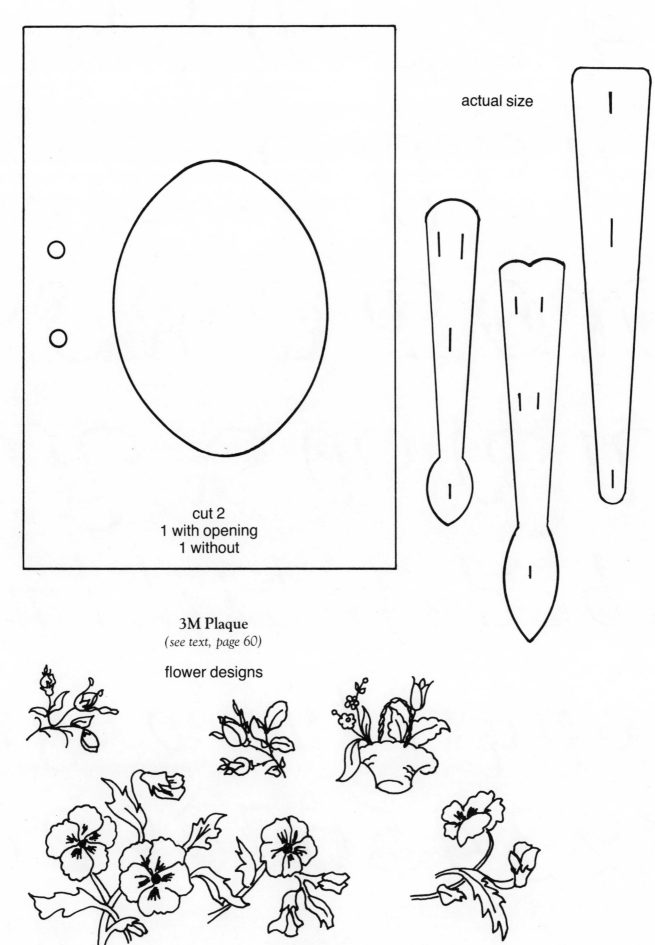

Floral Card
(moulded ornament, see text, page 59)

Fans
(moulded ornaments, see text, page 64)

actual size

cut 2
1 with opening
1 without

3M Plaque
(see text, page 60)

flower designs

A B C D E F G

H I J K L M

N O P Q R S T

U V W X Y Z

a b c d e f g h i j k l m n

o p q r s t u v w x y z

1 2 3 4 5 6 7 8 9 0 &

Floral Script

92

A B C D E F G H I

J K L M N O P Q R

S T U V W X Y Z

a b c d e f g h i j k l m

n o p q r s t u v w x y z

1 2 3 4 5 6 7 8 9 0th

&

Happy Birthday

Anniversary

Old English Text

93

A B C D E F G H I
J K L M N O P Q R
S T U V W X Y Z

a b c d e f g h i j k l m

n o p q r s t u v w x y z

1 2 3 4 5 6 7 8 9 0th

&

Happy Birthday

Anniversary

Park Avenue Script

94

INDEX

Numerals in roman denote text entry; in **bold**, photograph; in ***bold italic***, step-by-step photograph; in *italics*, pattern.